Ancient Secrets For Pets

and All Creatures Great & Small

Carol K. Ray

Wisdom of the World Press

ANCIENT SECRETS FOR PETS
AND ALL CREATURES GREAT & SMALL
by Carol K. Ray and the Ancient Secrets Community

with foreword by Dr. Clint G. Rogers
and Dr. Krushna Naram

Copyright© 2024 by Paul Clinton Rogers

All rights reserved.
No part of this book may be reproduced or stored in a retrieval system, or transmitted in any form or by any means, electronic, mechanical, photocopying, recording, or otherwise, without express written permission of the publisher.

Published by Wisdom of the World Press
www.MyAncientSecrets.com

ISBN: 978-1-952353-31-4
Book Cover Courtesy of Maryam Khalifah
Maryamart.illustration@gmail.com

Editing: Cornelia Merk
Interior design by Carol K. Ray
Printed in the United States

Medical Disclaimer

All content found in this document, printed or electronic, including text, images, audio, or other formats were created for informational purposes only. The Content is not intended to be a substitute for professional medical advice, diagnosis, or treatment. Always seek the advice of your physician or other qualified health provider with any questions you may have regarding a medical condition. Never disregard professional medical advice or delay in seeking it because of something you have read in this document.

If you think your pet may have a medical emergency, call your veterinarian or go to an animal emergency care facility. The Ancient Secrets Foundation does not recommend or endorse any specific tests, physicians, products, procedures, opinions, or other information that may be mentioned in this document. Reliance on any information provided by Ancient Secrets Foundation employees, volunteers, contracted writers, or medical professionals presenting content for publication is solely at your own risk.

Pets on prescription diets or medications should continue until you have discussed a change with your vet. Check with your vet first before changing the diet or treats for a pregnant or nursing pet, or introducing any sensitive pet to new foods, especially "people foods."

Always introduce foods slowly and in small quantities and watch for any reactions.

Foreword Dr. Clint G. Rogers

Dear One,

You picking up this book now says a lot about you, your heart, and how love is guiding you.

The original book that many of the Ancient Secrets principles in here have come from is called *'Ancient Secrets of a Master Healer'*. As that book has been translated into 30+ languages by volunteers (who simply want people they care about to have access to the material), I'm especially excited that the opening quote of that book is in every language and spread around the world:

"I didn't come to teach you. I came to love you. Love will teach you."

This book you are reading right now, *Ancient Secrets for Pets*, in many ways is living evidence of the power of this quote. And the fact that you were guided to it makes me so excited about what is likely about to happen in your life.

First, because love is embedded in the content, and second, in the way in which this book even came to be.

Regarding the content... for anyone who has ever had a connection with an animal, whether it be a dog or a cat or any other creature great or small, you very likely have learned some of your most powerful lessons in love through their presence in your life. I know that for sure happened for me, through the mystical appearance of the India street dog Milo in my life, just after Dr. Naram had left his body. I discovered through Milo how animals are so often our teachers, reflections of ourselves. Although that story is in this book, so I don't need to repeat it here, I do want to say that as you explore the Ancient Secrets more and more, you are likely going to see and experience even more of a mystical connection with all of life.

During my time with Dr. Naram, traveling the world, witnessing, and experiencing the profound healing power of these Ancient Secrets, I especially loved the moments when we would help animals.

I began as a skeptic, and I wondered if the healing for people would come mainly because of the 'placebo effect' - that they believed and that it was the power of their belief what healed them. Then, Dr. Naram would call me in and show me how to take the pulse of a dog, cat, horse, bird, snake, elephant, owl, monkey, tiger, and on and on. And it was magical to see how the Ancient Secrets would work for them, too! When I witnessed the Ancient Secrets work for babies, those in a coma, and for animals, it proved to me that the healing efficacy of the Ancient Secrets went far beyond placebo.

One thing that really challenged my academically trained way of looking at the world was when people would come for their own health challenge, and then Dr. Naram would prescribe as a part of their healing to feed animals. I would wonder, "how is their feeding of cows, dogs, or crows going to support their healing?" For several people struggling with certain mental challenges, like schizophrenia, Dr. Naram would prescribe that they feed fish every day, and watch the fish eat the food they placed in the water with their own hands. Dr. Naram would show me in the ancient manuscripts where this was recommended, and how it worked on principles beyond what most people in the western world ever consider.

Over time, I witnessed so many things that I could only describe as 'miracles', even though they were based on an ancient science. I began to realize there were many powerful impacts on physical, mental, emotional, and spiritual levels for any beings who came into contact with the Ancient Secrets.

Dr. Naram would teach me that all the elements that exist in nature also exist in all of us, and that when you discover where the imbalances and blocks are, that you can help resolve them... and that the natural state of any being is vibrant health. He also taught me that "everything is a medicine or poison depending on how use it," (*Ancient Secrets of a Master Healer*, Chapter 3, p. 55) - and that through learning these Ancient Secrets we could know how to help anyone, often with things in our own kitchens or homes. In this book, you'll discover many powerful stories of people who did this for animals in their lives; you'll learn exactly what were the remedies they used, and you'll enjoy what powerful results then came.

Beyond the clinic setting, Dr. Naram would always have us alert to how we treated any animals or life that crossed our paths. If we ever saw a stray dog, or a person or animal that was hungry, cold, or needed help... it was our blessing to do what we could to support. We would always have food in our car to give to anyone we saw in need, and after the end of very busy clinic days, sometimes at 3 am, we would then go out into the streets to put blankets on those who were homeless. There is a principle we would live by, called 'Atithi Devo Bhava' - which means to treat the unexpected guest as if God himself or herself has arrived. And this would include animals.

I used to think this was a cute but superstitious activity that Dr. Naram had us do. Now, after using this as a main principle during the 30-Day Miracle Experiment Game, an 'experiment' we have already guided thousands of people from around the world through, I see it as a very powerful & predictable secret science. If you apply this principle in your life consistently, you can unlock a different connection with all of life, which usually results in you seeing more mystical miracles of love and healing. If you want to have your own experience with this, definitely join us for the next Miracle Experience Game. As part of you purchasing this book, we want to give that 30-Day experience to you as a gift (see further down).

Through all of this, you will see how much love is woven through the content of this book, and how love will always be available to guide you, even in moments of greatest need.

Regarding the way this book came to exist, it has totally been guided and gifted by love. On March 8th 2020, Carol K Ray had a dream in which these powerful words came to her: "Heal yourself, and heal the world." She was just completing a very successful career in the corporate world and not sure what she was going to do next in her life, when this dream came. Shortly after, she came into contact with Sara Morrell, who introduced her to the Ancient Secrets of a Master Healer group, where a global Miracle Experiment Game was announced that had the slogan: "Heal yourself and heal the world."

Carol saw that as a sign, and for the last four years has been a dedicated student, wisdom collector, and keeper of the Ancient Secrets, which has resulted in first the *Ancient Secrets Cookbook*, and now this amazing book. And the way in which love guided her was not to do it alone, but through community. She reached out to the growing global Ancient Secrets community... and collected so many compelling stories, putting together this powerful book to bless animals, and all of us who love them.

And it is no accident that you found this book now.

Love guided you here.

Who knows how much contagious healing will come to you and through you, as you discover these Ancient Secrets?

And if you wish it to be, this book can be a starting point into a powerful world of many Ancient Secrets which can change your life forever. I will include a list of references below in the exciting possibility that you want to go further.

I'm so grateful you are here.

And I'm excited for how these Ancient Secrets can bless your life, and the lives of the animals you care for, as you let love guide you.

Much love and respect,
Dr. Clint G. Rogers

P.S. If you haven't read the book *'Ancient Secrets of a Master Healer'* yet, I'm excited for you to discover in it the principles behind why the remedies and secrets you'll find in this book are so effective. I'm also excited for you to read at the very end of that book the miracle experience that happened in Nepal at Swayambu ('the Monkey Temple'). It is a constant reminder to me of how all of life is connected, and how as we utilize the Ancient Secrets to tune us into love and into the flow of nature and all of life... so many mystical miracles of love and healing are possible.

Additional Resources for You

Miracle Experiment Game (30-days)

(FREE for those who purchase this book: https://www.MyAncientSecrets.com/petbookgift

Ancient Secrets Community

- Sunday Global Miracle Calls
  https://www.ancientsecretszoom.com

- Facebook group
  https://www.facebook.com/groups/MyAncientSecrets

- WhatsApp group
  https://chat.whatsapp.com/GD2HrBKHCphFSIXVVrZHsF

Courses to dive deeper into the Ancient Secrets

https://linktr.ee/drclintgrogers

Clinics / Consultations

To get on the waiting list for pulse clinics, and/or express interest in hosting a pulse clinic in your area, complete this form:

https://forms.gle/7AwjTJqK77wMkFzK6

Additional Books

- **Ancient Secrets of a Master Healer**

DISCOVER ANCIENT SECRETS THAT CAN CHANGE YOUR LIFE!

Join a skeptical university researcher from the USA as he travels to the Himalayas and uncovers secrets from an ancient healing lineage that began with Lord Buddha's physician.

For thousands of years, the greatest healers in the Himalayas have been refining a potent healing science for the treatment of physical ailments, psychological disorders and spiritual challenges. The most effective natural healing methods were recorded on ancient scrolls. Now, in this breakthrough, real-life account, many of these healing secrets are revealed by the author's encounters with legendary master healer Dr. Naram.

The secrets in this book can change your life forever.

https://www.amazon.com/Ancient-Secrets-Master-Healer-Greatest/dp/1952353009

- **Ancient Secrets Cookbook**

"If you change your food, you can change your future."

Are there diet secrets that help people live longer, healthier, & happier lives?

What if healthy eating could also be easy and delicious?

The *Ancient Secrets Cookbook* was inspired by Dr. Pankaj Naram and Dr. Clint G. Rogers PhD. Dr. Naram was a great healer who helped millions of people around the world by using Ancient Secrets from nature. Before he died, he passed on these secrets to his students, including Dr. Clint G. Rogers, who put many of them in his book, *Ancient Secrets of a Master Healer*.

This cookbook implements many of the ideas from the Ancient Secrets book and gives you ways to eat that do not cause pain and suffering. It's not easy cutting out gluten, refined sugar, dairy, and nightshade vegetables, but if you can change what you eat, you can change your life!

https://www.amazon.com/Ancient-Secrets-Cookbook-Recipes-Unlimited/dp/195235398X

- **Ancient Secrets for Kids**

Ancient Secrets for Kids Coloring and Activity Book was inspired by Dr. Pankaj Naram and Dr. Clint G. Rogers PhD.

The *Ancient Secrets Coloring and Activity Book* for Kid's invites children (of all ages) to think about what they want; what they want to be, as well as sharing insightful stories of using the natural healing power of herbs for animals and even insects!

https://www.amazon.com/Ancient-Secrets-Kids-Coloring-Activity/dp/1952353998

All three books have already been translated into various languages by volunteers.

Foreword Dr. Krushna Naram

Namaskar, namaskar! Welcome, welcome. I love you. And I am with you. My name is Dr. Krushna Pankaj Naram. I am the son of Dr. Pankaj Naram and Dr. Smita Naram. And with Big News!

The fact that you are here, reading this, is powerful. I welcome all of you.

Carol is doing some powerful work and believe it or not, in the next few pages, the Ancient Secrets that you can discover, and you WILL DISCOVER, can be life changing.

Discover ancient secrets of deeper healing beyond species. How to connect with your loved animals, how to connect with animals in a way they love you back and they feel understood. And what are the principles, lost Ancient Secrets of healing any animal from their pain? Discover how you can go from misery and illness to bliss, and even going beyond wellness, beyond joy, and bring deeper, lasting healing.

Carol, I wish you all the best for this beautiful book. And I'm with you in this for sharing these methods, these deep secrets from thousands of years which have been with us and finally available to the world. I love you and I am with you.

Namaskar.

Dr. Krushna Naram

About this Book

Ancient Secrets for Pets & All Creatures Great and Small

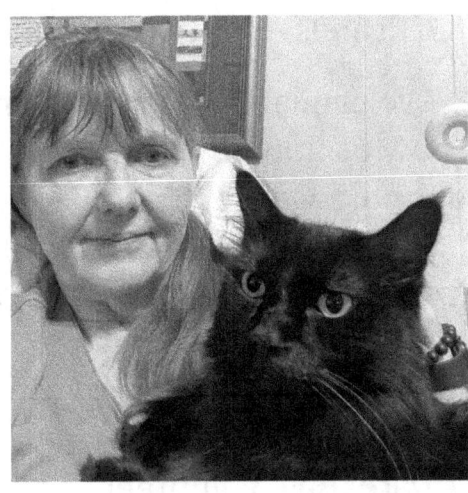

When Dr. Clint G. Rogers published his book *Ancient Secrets of a Master Healer*, it touched on some of the incredible stories of Dr. Pankaj Naram's success with healing an elephant, helping a Bengal Tiger, treating a kangaroo, and even how Dr. Giovanni Brincivalli saved a bee colony from a virus. *Ancient Secrets for Pets* focuses on using the same principles and techniques for our fur babies: dogs, cats, and rabbits, as well as horses, birds, reptiles, even insects! All God's creatures great and small, and all things wise and wonderful can benefit from the Ancient Secrets.

In times of crisis when vets and supplies like dog and cat food might not be available, it's a good idea to know which herbal remedies are safe for pets, how to make your own pet food, which table foods are dangerous and which ones heal. We ask that you take time to think through what evacuation with your pets might entail to have a plan in advance. As an evacuee from a huge New Mexico fire in 2021, I know how stressful and emotional these events can be. Have a plan: it could make a huge difference in the outcome of events such as wild fires, tornadoes, hurricanes, typhoons, earthquakes, etc.

We can learn so much from our pets: they show us how to be in the present, how to express unbridled joy, even how to forgive and love unconditionally. We hope you find *Ancient Secrets for Pets and All Creatures Great and Small* to be informative, engaging, and inspiring.

I love you and I am with you,

Carol Ray, Volunteer
Ancient Secrets Community

Contents

Medical Disclaimer iii
Foreword Dr. Clint G. Rogers v
Foreword Dr. Krushna Naram xv
    About this Book xvii
Master Jivaka. 1
Healing Stories from Dr. Naram 3
    Dr. Krushna Naram – Animals & Ancient Secrets 4
    Dipika Delmenico – Animal Stories of Dr. Naram 16
    Transmuting Fear into Love (of SNAKES!) 16
    Dr. Naram and the Kangaroos 19
    Dr. Giovanni Brincivalli & the Rabbit 22
Stories of Ancient Secrets Helping Pets 25
    Dr. Naram - Dog with a Tumor 26
    Dr. Clint G. Rogers and Milo 28
    Dr. Giovanni & the Dog with a Bleeding Problem . . . 31
    Dr. Giovanni Brincivalli & the Dog, Martino 32
    Levi Lieske and Rosco 33
    Carol Ray and Osi 36
    Lisa Lowe - Dr. Naram to the Rescue 41
    Esther Wolkowitz and Mamacita 45
    Jayna Taylor and Oakley 49
    Punam Patel: Reiki and Luna 55
    Dr. Stephen Wechsler & Hank 59
    Mirayah & Street Dogs in India 64
    Mike and the Pashupatinath Dogs of Nepal 65

Ancient Secrets & Horses..........67
Peggy Coleman Taylor: We Owe so Much to Horses . . 68
Ann Wilkinson's Horse Stories 70
Ayurveda & Horses 75

Ancient Secrets and Birds 77
Carol K. Ray: Birds, Vultures, and Energy 78
Dr. Giovanni Brincivalli & the Eagle.........84

Emergencies & Pets 87
Essential Oils & Cats & Dogs 89
Mindy Barrett: Evacuating with Pets 93

Helping Your Pet To Heal 101
Six Instruments of Siddha-Veda 102
Pets and Siddha-Veda - Ayurveda 103
What are Doshas 104
Vata Dosha in Animals 106
Pitta Dosha in Animals 109
Kapha Dosha in Animals 110

Herbs for Cats & Dogs 119
Turmeric 120
Tulsi 121
Ashwagandha and Neem............121
Triphala 123
Cannabis 123

Remedies for Pets 125
Cat Eye Infection 126
Constipation 126
Diarrhea..................126
Ear Issues 127

Fleas & Ticks 128
  Insect Bites 128
  Separation Anxiety 129
  Vomiting, Belching, and Burping. 130
  Pets Seizures - Fits & Shakes 131

Pets & Skin Conditions. **135**
  Abscesses 136
  Mast Cell Tumors 136
  Sebaceous Cyst 137
  Skin is Too Dry 137

Dietary Recommendations **139**
  Diet for Your Dog 141
  Safe & Natural Pet Food 142
  Special Diet for Sick and/or Elderly Cats (Baby Food) . 145
  Unsafe Foods for Pets 148

Making Your Own Dog Food - Lisa Lowe . . . **153**
  Homemade Dog Kibble 154
  Recipes for Cardiovascular Issues 159
  Dogs with Kidney issues 164

Our Final Gift - Dr. Susan Engman **169**

Charities We Love That Support Animals . . . **175**

References **181**

Index **184**

Ancient Secrets Community **191**

Book Cover Design **192**

Master Jivaka

Master Jivaka said everything can be either a poison or a medicine, depending on how you use it.

The same can be said for the food we feed our pets.

What provides nourishment for one might cause suffering for another.

You can make an appointment for yourself or your pets with Dr. Clint G. Rogers if he is coming to a place near you by applying at this link: https://www.MyAncientSecrets.com/contact-us/

You can make an appointment for a zoom call at Ayushakti here: https://www.AncientSecretsFoundation.org/Consultation

Either will guide you forward to the correct dietary recommendations, and potentially herbs for you, and often help with your fur babies. To live with vibrant health is the greatest accomplishment in life.

Without a healthy body, a sound mind and emotional tranquility, all other aspects of our lives will be negatively impacted. Our intention for sharing with you the gift of Siddha-Veda lifestyle is only to empower you, and not to limit you.

To become independent and free of disease one needs inspiration, guidance, and an understanding of how our body (and our pets) responds to certain foods, lack of sleep, our environment, relationships, social life, too much or too little physical activities, daily schedule, and so on.

Discover the book *Ancient Secrets of a Master Healer: A Western Skeptic, An Eastern Master, And Life's Greatest Lessons.*
https://www.MyAncientSecrets.com

Healing Stories from Dr. Naram Practitioners & Vaidyas

Dr. Krushna Naram – Animals & Ancient Secrets

Are ancient secrets of deeper healing beyond species? How can you connect with your beloved animals, connect with animals in a way where they love you back and they feel understood? And what are the lost principles of ancient secrets for healing any animal from their pain? How can we help others to go from misery to bliss, from illness, going beyond wellness, beyond joy, and bringing deeper, lasting healing?

I invite you to take notes on things you can implement in YOUR life. Be prepared because you will really discover deep, powerful secrets, methods, mantras, Marmaas, home remedies, herbal remedies, lifestyle secrets, and even panchakarma for your animals - for a dog, cat, horse, honeybees, butterflies, lion, tiger, python, or elephant. I leave it up to your imagination.

Now follow these methods as they are because they come from a lineage which is over 2500 years old. They have been used by the physician of the Buddha (Jivaka) and they have been used by my father, my mother, and me. And they make a difference, no matter what.

Let me share with you a true, very amazing, and inspiring story. It is beautiful. And it is just heart melting. Heartwarming. Most of you know my father,

Dr. Pankaj Naram, and my mother, Dr. Smita Naram, have been practicing for the last 35 to 40 years, in about 160 countries, helping about one and a half million people. And in his lifetime, my father saw about 10 million pulses; out of this, there were hundreds of thousands of people and animals who would come to him to show him their pulse. Really!

What are the ancient secrets of helping animals?

This all began in a powerful way in 1994 or 1995, when for the first time, a man came to my father. At that time, he didn't have a very big clinic. He didn't have this three-floor building where he could help people in a powerful way. He had a smaller clinic, and he was just beginning his professional life. At this time there would be about a hundred to sometimes three hundred people coming to him. There was one man who came who was particularly distinctive. You would notice him. You could point him out in the crowd.

He was strong, tall, well shaved, well maintained, with a fit physique and he looked very kind. Even a different sparkle was in his eyes, a joy from inside, as if he was experiencing the joy of service; but he didn't look like someone who was a monk or a someone who had left everything behind and just went into a life of renunciation.

He was in the world now. He's waiting and he comes in and Papa sees his pulse. He says, "Oh my

God, you are a very good man. But there is a lot of stress and anxiety inside, which is why you are getting high blood pressure, fatty liver, cholesterol, borderline diabetes, HBA 1C will be around 6.46. And you are not having a good relationship with your wife right now, and your children are being agitated because of that, and you are losing hair, and your mother had this, father had that, and your children can get these after 15 years."

The man was amazed. He says, "Dr. Naram, Dr. Smita Naram, how can you do this? What do I do? You're absolutely right: 100%. What do I do?"

And then Papa made a plan with a diet, lifestyle, Marmaa, home remedies, herbal supplements, and panchakarma; Mom and Dad crafted this together. Ultimately, he followed it diligently for six months. And believe it or not, at the end of six months, he says, "I was very muscular. I used to exercise a lot, had good muscle strength, but there was something missing. I would feel tired and irritated suddenly. It wouldn't show up on my face, but inside myself, I knew it. Dr. Naram, Dr. Smita, the last six months have changed my life. I feel like a new person. My life is changed. I love my wife and she loves me more. I love my children. My children love me more. The family is closer together. Dr. Naram, because you changed my life, I want to give you one experience which can be just thrilling, which can change YOUR life."

And Papa got excited because he felt something exciting coming!

Then the man says, "Dr. Naram, I am the Forest Officer, head of the entire forest called the Mumbai Area Forest. I live next to the Area Forest, so there are leopards that sometimes come near my house, as well as snakes, birds, all sorts of different, wonderful beings."

So this man is the head in charge of that entire forest!

"I want to give you an intimate experience with something dangerous."

Papa said, "Okay, but what kind of dangerous experience?"

"Come, come to this address, at this time."

Papa goes to that place. It's in the center of the forest. And the man says "Very good. You are here, Dr. Naram. Come, good doctor, I want to take you somewhere special," and he enters a lane which is full of cages on either side. There, in captivity, are lions, lionesses, leopards, cheetahs, tigers, and Papa is blown away. He's at a 2-3 feet distance from these majestic beings, these amazing mighty cats.

He's just watching them, and they're watching him. They're roaring! He can hear them breathe. That's how close he was with them, and he's absolutely thrilled.

And then the man says, "Dr. Naram, we need your help."

Papa says, "Okay." But what could it be?

The man says, "Look, you saw my pulse and you made sure I had an empty stomach. And you saw my pulse and I asked you why an empty stomach was required. You said that food spoils the pulse. You cannot understand it. You cannot have a proper pulse reading experience if you're eating food because it changes the outcome. I said okay, and came with an empty stomach. And you were spot on. Now we have a problem, and we want your help. We have a patient who needs you."

People aren't typically allowed to go in the place where Papa was just welcomed so openly, with so much love and protection. He says, "Okay, I'm here for you or whomever."

They go a little further and he sees this lioness crammed in a tinier cage than all the others and a little bit agitated, just lying down. Anyone comes close and she would roar; she would make these sounds like she did not like it. The noise irritated her. Papa looks at her. He asked, "What happened to her? What do you want me to do?"

"This is the patient," the Forest Officer says.

What? Everybody just says, what?

And he says, "Dr. Naram, do you remember how you made me come with an empty stomach because of the pulse reading? I wanted to do the best I can. We haven't given her any food and she's really hungry! Usually when she sees a vet, we sedate her. But I know it would have changed the pulse. She's not sedated and she's extremely hungry."

Papa says, "Ohh God, are you crazy? Oh my God. Here's this lioness who's been hungry for a couple of days, not sedated, alert and really angry, irritated, and you want me to see the pulse of her? It's okay to keep people hungry, but really, you could have fed her, no problem. What if she bites me? It's my hand! My work depends on these three fingers to see the Vata, Pitta, and Kapha. I cannot. Oh my God."

But then he gets into a state of just **being.**

So that's the first secret. (Write it down!)

There are three primary states: knowing, doing, and being. When you **know** something, then you're in your head; when you are too much in **doing**, then you are doing, doing, doing, but not stopping, listening, thinking, and you're just doing. You may be doing right or wrong, good or bad, whatever things that are working for you or not working for you, but you're **doing.**

And then there's **being**, when you're in the present, you're centered. You work from a place of love where you do when needed and don't do when it's not needed. Know what to do, how to do, and it is a deeper state of **being**.

Papa went into his state of knowing, doing and being, and IN being, oh, dear me, he went back to his master; many years back, maybe 15 or 20 years back when he met his master and to the 1000 days of training. His master took Mommy and Papa to many experiences, especially with animals, and Papa recalled being sent to Nepal to meet with another master who was 115 years young at the time.

Jnaneddrajii & Carol Ray, April 2023 in the Pashpatinanth Ashram. Master Chun Chun Baba top right.

Chun Chun Baba gave Papa and Mommy many miracle experiences. Papa thought back to those experiences and he recalled a Mantra which helps to connect with the spirit of animals and connect beyond language. When a Being doesn't know, or doesn't have a perception of what we call language, how do you reach out to their heart and bring deeper healing?

Papa remembered all that, and Mom and Dad got in their "Being." Papa starts saying the mantra. The moment he comes close to the lioness she feels like, "Who is this encroaching on my space? It's already a tiny cage!"

But then Papa begins saying this mantra over and over, over, and over, while doing a specific Marmaa on himself. Then all of a sudden there is a connection. Barriers melt away. There is an open space of communication, of love, and of healing.

Now he slowly comes close to the lioness, and the lioness knows he doesn't want to harm her, but wants to understand her. He wants to be with her, he wants to give her love and get back the love. And there is a connection. He slowly goes to her, holds her paw. Touches the pulse. Closes his eyes, feels into it. So does Mom. And now Papa comes back, and he says to the Forest Officer, "Thank you for this experience."

The Forest Officer says, "Yes, this was magical. She calmed down. She never does that. She is known to be the most aggressive! Amazing, but what is it? What did you find, Dr. Naram?" He was so excited to find out.

Papa says, "Look, the lioness is having some kind of a mental challenge. She's feeling depressed and angry because of her depression."

The Forest Officer says, "I don't get it. What do you mean? How can a lion feel depressed? What else?"

"She is suffering from infertility. She cannot conceive. The main cause of her depression is because she wants to be a mother. But there is a tubal block."

The man is blown away because recently a vet confirmed that the lioness has a tubal block. Now, what to do? So Papa says this is the diet. Here is the home remedy and herbal supplements. Everything is necessary.

The caretaker is listening to all this, and says, "I'm quitting my job! You are telling me I have to go to the lioness and do the Marmaa? I'm not going to do it. Are you crazy? Dr. Naram can do whatever he wants to do. I'm not doing it! I don't get paid enough to do this!"

Now, how do we give the herbs? Papa says you have to feed the herbs twice a day. The caretaker says, "Are you crazy? I'm going to put my hand in her MOUTH and then FEED her the herbs??? No WAY!!!"

So they think about what to do. Finally, they come up with the idea of making slits inside the raw meat that she eats and put the tablets inside that. And that's how they began.

Over a period of two, three months, she started to be calmer, happier, less reactive to people coming close to her. Unbelievable, but still, there was no big result because still she was not pregnant. Six months, nine months passed, and Papa forgot about it. Mommy forgot about it.

Then one day this tall man entered the office. Dr. Naram says, "Oh. Forest Officer, how are you? Please. Welcome. Welcome."

He comes and he says "Dr. Naram, I'm so happy to see you. I have a big surprise for you."

And he got Mommy and Papa and took them to the same place they were almost a year before. And now they're seeing this lioness, and she turns around; they go on the other side. They see these tiny, beautiful cubs! Oh my goodness, Papa and Mommy's heart melted.

And that's the deeper healing the lion got in her life, the joy of being a mother. Suddenly she was loving everybody. She was not angry, agitated. She would not roar unexpectedly. She had a sense of connection with people. This was amazing!

There have been stories of pythons, monkeys, crocodiles, alligators, kangaroos, wolves, owls, eagles, all of them who've been helped, and the principle of helping is the same.

My dear ones. Write down the second secret. The second secret is the principle of *Loka Purusha Samya Siddhanta Pande Tat Bramante Siddhanta.*

It means what exists outside exists inside and so if the outside world is infinite, the inside world is infinite and the outside world is a reflection of the inner world.

Now the principle is that all of us are indeed connected and made with the same stuff. Therefore, what works for humans are the same principles through which animals, trees, birds, fish, all of them can be helped. This is the principle. This is the Ancient Secret. Now you have it.

And now for the mantra: what was the mantra that allowed Papa to break the barrier and connect with the spirit of the lioness? What was the mantra that allowed this communication to happen?

This was given to me by Papa in 2011. It's been with me ever since. And the moment I did it, miracles just happened. I've seen it. I've experienced it, so I encourage you. Go ahead immediately try this out. Your life will change. Are you ready for this?

Sit straight, keep your spine straight. Breathe in with your nose, take a deep breath. Exhale through your mouth, inhale through your nose, and out with your mouth. With open ears, say out loud:

Om Sham (pronounced SHOM) Namaha

Do this again and again, again and again when you are with the animal and Papa would say, that's what is important. You love the animal.

That's one thing: you love. The animal is one thing. The animal feels that it loves you: that is the second thing; and the animal loves you back is the third thing. When these three things happen, then deeper healing can take place and this mantra helps bridge the gap so that these three things can happen, and a deeper healing connection can happen.

Many amazing stories and miracles have happened throughout my life. Now there is one thing I want to leave you with. It is a Marmaa.

What is the Marmaa to help bring this mantra power even deeper?

With the fingers of your right hand, index finger and thumb, with the nails of the fingers, rub the nails together on that hand and same with the left-hand index finger and thumb. Rub the nails together while saying the mantra.

You may or may not hear the sound, but the animals will feel the vibration. It's very mild. But it works. These two together make a big difference. There are many powerful ancient secrets, and let's get on this journey together.

Dipika Delmenico – Animal Stories of Dr. Naram

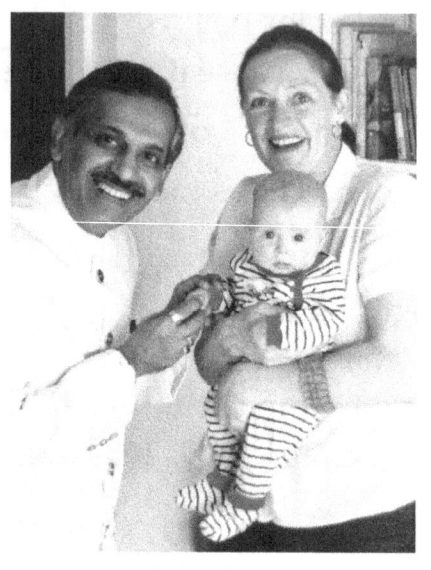

Here are two short stories that I wish to share about personal experiences that I've had the great fortune of having and sharing with Dr. Pankaj Naram, involving being in service to, and the care of animals. While I had many experiences with animals and Dr. Naram, these are two that I wish to share and the first is a story regarding taking care of patients; in an animal form... as snakes.

Transmuting Fear into Love (of SNAKES!)

I grew up in a country town in Australia on the edge of bush land where there were venomous snakes. Australia has many venomous snakes! As a child I loved to play in the bush with my friends. You could find me running through the bush knowing that whether I could see them or not, there were venomous snakes about. I was always told to be careful in summertime and to be on the lookout for snakes. I grew up with a respectful fear of snakes.

On becoming a parent, living on a rural bush property with highly venomous brown snakes and tiger snakes, I became vigilant about my children being snake aware, as they played and ran through long grass and bush bare foot. My fear of snakes lived on.

In between my childhood and having children I had the incredible experience of taking the pulse of a few snakes.

One day in Ayushakti Malad Clinic in Mumbai, India, with Dr. Naram, several patients came in and they were snakes. Dr. Naram said that we were going to treat the snakes as patients and take the pulse of snakes, and it was a really great way to address our own fear.

So I took the pulse of snakes, and it was beautiful! It was amazing to feel the texture of the skin. To feel the body temperature of the snake. And to feel the sensations as they came through my fingertips!

The pulse expresses what was happening with the snake and its biological humors just like the pulse of all creatures and living beings. On reading the pulse we could tell what was happening with the health of the snake.

With the first snake, there was a problem with humidity and dampness (Bhej) which was creating health challenges. The snake had a cold with a cough.

Another snake that day had skin problems. It had a skin wound that had to be treated.

One of Dr. Naram's assistants was directed by Dr. Naram to apply a healing skin balm to the wound and affected site. He was applying a balm made of medicated ghee and various Ayurvedic herbs. The herbs were crushed and mixed into the ghee and applied to the snake's skin.

He was so present! He had No Fear whatsoever. His love for this creature was really evident. It was tangible.

The snake was fully receptive to receiving the therapeutic gesture and the one offering it in LOVE. It was amazing to witness as the snake moved his head around and came up close to the therapist assistant. It was moving its tongue about, flickering it against the therapist who was fully focused and did not flinch or recoil at all from the snake. There was a stunning communion occurring.

Dr. Naram said, "Look. Do you see? He is serving the snake with love and the snake feels it and is responding with love."

It was such a beautiful experience because I moved from the perception that "snakes will harm you" to one of LOVE... and reverence for the beauty, the majesty, of this living creature.

Dr. Naram and the Kangaroos

In the early 2000's on one of Dr. Naram's Australian clinic tours, he really had a yearning to take the pulse of kangaroos: he so wished to take the pulse of kangaroos! And so one of our colleagues, a friend of ours and a friend of our Ayushakti clinics in Australia, arranged for us to visit a small private Wildlife Refuge run by a woman in the hills outside to the east of Melbourne (Australia). We drove out to visit this small animal refuge where orphaned Kangaroos (the orphaned babies are called joeys) and injured Kangaroos were cared for, where they were housed. Dr. Naram was so excited!

Here we were, not only driving through a beautiful landscape and environment but also we drove up this hill, up this winding, long dirt driveway to reach this property. It was really beautiful!

I remember this drive distinctly because I felt some panic due to the bottom of my car scraping on this rough driveway. And I thought oh, this doesn't sound good. Have I lost my muffler? Will we actually make it home?

Nevertheless, we arrived and Dr. Naram was so excited to step into this home where there were about a dozen or more Kangaroos being cared for at this particular moment; some were adult Kangaroos. There were many joeys, baby Kangaroos. They have a little hammock-like cradle made for them, and it's warm, and they're cocooned in it so that it replicates the warmth and the environment of the mother's pouch.

Dr. Naram was in his element to be able to offer care to the Kangaroos that were not well, and to understand Kangaroos more fully through having taken their pulse.

The first thing he said when he took the pulse of the first kangaroo was whoa! So much Vata! And of course there is a great deal of movement and activity with Kangaroos!

He got to hold and nurse baby joeys, and he prescribed some dietary advice and some remedies to support those who had health challenges and really needed support.

It was just such a beautiful day, and it was a great moment for him. It really was realizing a vision that he wished to create by taking the pulse of Kangaroos. And not only taking the pulse of Kangaroos, but then working with Kangaroos as patients.

Of course it illustrates that whether it's a human being, a plant, an animal, a lethal creature that can inject deadly venom into somebody, or one that is domesticated or wild: all are living beings possessing qualities of the Divine. And we have the opportunity to serve the Divine in them.

In this way, we experience the Divine in US! And really contribute through our whole loving presence, to all of humanity. It's a living illustration of love teaching us. Being here, love, and love teaching us.

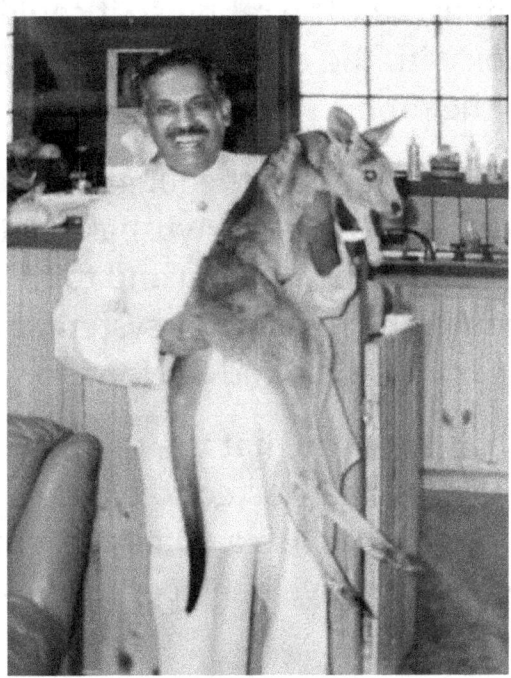

Dr. Naram in Australia,
joyously tending to Kangaroos

Dr. Giovanni Brincivalli & the Rabbit

A lady once brought a rabbit to see me and told me the vet had diagnosed the rabbit with severe BPCO (a breathing disorder similar to COPD) and this was confirmed with an X-Ray (tomography). The owner had noticed that the rabbit was breathing much faster than usual, which led to the appointment with the vet and the identification of the chronic problem.

The vet prescribed inhalation therapy for the rabbit – according to the owner, this was accomplished by putting the aromatic medication in a box big enough for the rabbit so it could inhale the air in the box with the therapeutic medication but it didn't help the rabbit.

As a remedy to support the lungs, I gave the rabbit Divyaswas Jivan from Ayushakti, intended to support the respiratory system and to help reduce inflammation in the respiratory system, as well as Asthtaloc for circulation and Hartone for circulation.

I was so happy to see that the rabbit was smelling the herbal tablets and started to eat them by himself! For me it was like a quality test of the herbs! These herbs have been certified as pure by the rabbit!

Dr. Clint with a little white rabbit

Watercolor by Elissa Ray: 11/1/2022

"Our two greatest obstacles in life (to seeing ourselves and others clearly) are ego and fear."

Dr. Pankaj Naram

From *Ancient Secrets of a Master Healer,* p. 75

Stories of Ancient Secrets Helping Pets And Their People

Dr. Naram - Dog with a Tumor

Featuring Michael and Super Dog, Angel

Video Link: Dr. Pankaj Naram Secret for Tumor? - YouTube

In the video above, Dr. Naram shares how a tumor due to Cushing's Disease and inoperable was reduced with herbal supplements.

After the dog was examined by a doctor, the tumor was only marginally identifiable. The dog is very happy and healthy for a 15-year-old! Dr. Naram's Ancient Healing methods can often reduce tumors.

The secrets Dr. Pankaj Naram is sharing were discovered 2500 years ago, initiated by Master Jivaka, physician to the Buddha, and passed down through the Siddha-Veda lineage, master to master. The guiding principle is finding the cause of the illness, rather than the symptoms causing it. Once the cause is understood, balance can be restored through a combination of remedies, herbal supplements, and other Ancient Secrets.

Home Remedy for Tumors

Anti-Tumor: Turmeric – Ginger – Black Pepper

- Turmeric powder: 1 tsp.
- Ginger juice: 1 tsp.
- Holy Basil: 7-11 leaves
- Black pepper: 3 peppercorns (crushed)
- Ghee: 1 teaspoon cows' ghee

Mix it all together and give it twice daily if there is any tumor. Start with a small amount for a pet, ¼ teaspoon, and gradually increase by 1/8 teaspoon, depending on your pet's age and weight.

Dr. Clint G. Rogers and Milo

On the morning after the prayer service for Dr. Naram at about 5:30 a.m. I woke up feeling especially lost and lonely. A dark cloud of an oncoming depression started to cast over my mind. It was still dark outside, too, but I couldn't sleep. So, I got out of bed, put my shoes on and went for a walk. Twenty minutes into my aimless wander, I suddenly became aware that someone was following me. At first it startled me, but then I saw it was a dog. He had brown legs, head, and tail, with black fur on his back, almost like a coat. His belly and a good portion of his nose were white. When I stopped to look at him, he stopped to look at me. When I continued walking, he followed closely behind. I was bewildered. Why was this dog following me?

I didn't have any food with me, and my hands were empty. It was a long walk and no matter which way I turned or what path I took, this dog stayed with me. It was both amusing and confusing.

Breaking through my sadness came this thought; I remembered Dr. Naram always had something for dogs or anyone that came to him. I heard his voice in my mind say, 'Atithi Devo Bhava.' (Treat the unexpected guest as if God/Goddess himself/herself has come to visit you.) As the sun rose and shops opened, I bought some biscuits for this unexpected visitor, as he patiently sat on the ground and waited for me.

However, when I placed the biscuits on the ground in front of him, the dog sniffed them and then looked back up at me without taking a bite or even so much as licking them.

In a little bit of frustration, I blurted out, "What do you want then?"

I started to walk away, and the dog followed me... for over an hour as I wandered the streets. As the mystery of this dog's appearance worked on me, some of the darkness started to lift. It was as if Dr. Naram's voice came into my mind and heart, reminding me of ancient secrets and truths I had learned during our time together, but now I understood in a deeper way.

That night, when the dog was still with me, I didn't know what to do when I tried to thank the dog for the gift of his appearance that day, and tried to close the door to my apartment -- and the dog started barking really loud. It was with very cautious concern that I opened the door again, and stepped to the side as the dog walked into my apartment. In fact, the only way the dog wouldn't bark was if he slept on the floor right next to me, with my hand on his head.

That mystical meeting changed the course of my life... and inspired the original Miracle Experiment Game, which now thousands of people around the world have played.

Dr. Clint G. Rogers and Milo after a walk together

And then for almost 6 months as the pandemic shut down airports and travel opportunities, this dog was my faithful companion and teacher as I published the book *Ancient Secrets of a Master Healer* and witnessed all the miracles associated with that, including the movement to translate it into 30+ languages.

Dr. Giovanni & the Dog with a Bleeding Problem

A female dog was having a problem with low blood platelets (thrombocytopenia), which caused a rapid heartbeat and excessive bleeding. The owner had to protect the furniture with material so that the dog would not be injured by the edges of the furniture. It was taken to the University where they detected the blood platelet disorder. They even gave the dog blood transfusions.

Our remedy for this situation was the following Herbal Remedies from Ayushakti:

Raktabandha – for slowing blood flow

Pittashamak – for digestive issues

Jivanjog – Immune booster

The dog fully recovered, lived many more years, without any bleeding problems.

Dr. Giovanni Brincivalli & the Dog, Martino

Martino was a small sized and very active dog who loved to go for walks before he was diagnosed with heart failure. He was also suffering from stiff joints, so much so that he was no longer able to jump up on the sofa. When he was carefully put on the sofa, he was unwilling to make even the small jump down.

Marino was put on a diet of moong bean soup (no onions or garlic), as well as herbal supplements from Ayushakti, specifically Sandhiyog, an anti-inflammatory for the joints, and Jivan Rakshak – a strong heart formula.

After a few months, Martino was back to his active self, regained his vitality, and is once again able to jump on the sofa and back down again, and to again join his owner on walks.

Martino continued to love eating moong bean soup. When they once had another dog as a guest, everyone was surprised that the guest also enjoyed the moong bean soup!

Levi Lieske and Rosco

In April 2020, amid the COVID lockdown, my beloved dog Rosco, a Pitbull, faced a health crisis. Due to heightened precautions and breed-based fears, he was heavily sedated and given a rabies vaccine during a routine X-ray of his paw. This treatment unexpectedly revealed a hidden blessing: it aggravated a previously undetected mass in his stomach, visible on an ultrasound as a plum-sized growth pressing on his internal organs, hindering his ability to defecate.

Rosco's condition was dire, with his temperature soaring to a perilous 104.5 degrees and constant trembling from pain. The vet's grim prognosis and the suggestion of a costly and risky surgery left me in a state of despair. However, inspired by stories of miraculous recoveries through natural remedies, I embarked on a bold, alternative path to healing.

I learned about a Polish doctor's success in reversing ailments with organic raw vegetable juices and a similar case where a heart tumor in a dog was treated this way. Rosco, unable to eat but willing to drink, was given alkalized water and a concoction of beet juice, burdock root, ginger, broccoli, radish, spinach, parsley, and black seed oil, using a turkey baster. This concoction aimed at alkalizing his body and countering the acidic effects of the vaccine and sedation.

As Rosco struggled, my heart was heavy with guilt and worry. Sitting beside him, a moment of a shared gaze shifted my mindset from fear to hope. I turned to my gratitude journal, envisioning Rosco healthy and vibrant, as he once was in the past... using my visualization, remembering when Roscoe was healthy, and what that looked like, and how it felt to play with him. This practice transformed my fear into hopeful anticipation.

Remarkably, on the sixth day of this regimen, Rosco's temperature began to drop. He started eating again, and soon after, on about day 6 (faith and true hope was required here), his temperature went down and he was finally being able to defecate, which led to a significant reduction in the stomach mass.

Before long, Rosco was back to his playful self, jumping and galloping, just as I had visualized in my journal. This journey of healing, now three and a half years past, remains a profound testament to hope, natural healing, and the unbreakable bond between a pet and their owner.

"No matter how big the problem or difficulty, never give up hope."

Baba Ramdas, Dr. Naram's Master
From *Ancient Secrets of a Master Healer*, p. 190

Carol Ray and Osi

The ancient secrets show us that we are so much more effective if we give our 100%. No multitasking. Just put your phone down, be in the present and give 100% attention to the task at hand.

This was a powerful lesson for me. It made a tangible difference in the relationship with my fur baby, Osi. He is a special need, inbred pup that I adopted at 5 weeks old when his young red heeler mother stopped nursing him. She was only 7 months old when she gave birth following an unplanned pregnancy from the neighboring farm's Catahoula. This intruder is not only Osi's parent, but also his grandfather!

Catahoula, named for a lake in the state of Louisiana, is a strong working dog, often used for killing feral hogs on Texas ranches, and known for their physical strength.

Osi demonstrated his aggression when only a few months old. He has a Pitta Dosha and is definitely an alpha male. He was less than a year old the first time he bit me badly, which was territorial and due to him having an undetected bladder infection. It took two grown men to carry him in his kennel into the vet, with him snarling, growling, and attacking his cage.

The vet prescribed antibiotics but recommended putting him down (terminating his life) because of his aggression. She would not treat him again and doubted any vet would treat him.

It took a great deal of courage to work through his healing, but we did it. I took him to a dog training school, but the trainer let him choke himself on his collar and leash as she pulled up the leash, putting pressure on his neck! I couldn't stand it and said she wasn't the trainer he needed.

I don't give up on people or pets just because they are difficult. I found a loving trainer who has a Catahoula, and he taught me first to read the dog's body language: watch the position of his ears, the position of the tail and overall position. Osi was a quick study and loved learning. He mastered going to his place, sit, stay, leave it, lay down, play dead, fetch, drop, speak, whisper, and more. He is now 10 years old, has never had an accident in the house, has saved me 3 times from rattlesnakes, and makes me laugh on a regular basis at his antics. He has lost control 4 times, biting.

The third incident happened in 2021 because I had the nail clippers out and touched his toe with my finger. His bites caused nasty wounds on my arms and legs. My soul was hurting from what felt like a betrayal of my best friend.

He was so sorry. He could hardly make eye contact. He wasn't eating. When offered a treat, he hesitated, then looked away. Looked back, looked at me, licked my hand, and very, very gently took the treat from my hand and slowly walked away.

My spirits were still so low days later. I reached out for support from Dr. Clint G. Rogers, author of *Ancient Secrets of a Master Healer*, whose community bound by love was where I spent my free time volunteering to serve in whatever capacity I could. I told him my wounds and bruises would heal, but I was really struggling with fear.

He said he knew someone well who is an amazing Reiki Master for animals. He gave me the name, and I called and made an appointment for Osi. I am very familiar with the powerful healing power of Reiki even though I didn't have experience with Reiki for pets.

The session went very well. I sat nearby, holding space, sending love to my beloved Osi. At first, he was sighing and breathing shallowly. He seemed to relax after a few minutes and turned to his side. His breathing slowed, and he seemed receptive.

After the session, I received a call from the Reiki Master that at first Osi was not interested in the session. He called himself a bad dog and said he didn't know how it happened; he just lost control. He was oh so sorry.

After the report, she said, there is a soul here needing some help. It's ___, do you know someone on this plane with that name? I said yes, she's part of our Ancient Secrets Community. She was enrolled in a class but struggling with depression and illness.

After giving Osi some dedicated time, petting him, loving on him, he went outside and I sent a text to the person whose name had come up in the Reiki session for Osi. She called and we had a wonderful heart to heart talk. She confided that much of her pain stemmed from physical abuse as a child when she was given to an orphanage because her mom could not afford to take care of her. The abuse started at a very young age, and unfortunately continued when she was adopted. She ran away from home at a young age.

Her story was almost exactly the same as the story of Denny Dalkin, may she rest in peace, who wrote a book about her story called, 'Love is the Only Truth.' I was able to arrange a counseling session for the suffering woman whose spirit showed up at the Reiki session for Osi that was helping me heal from my fear!

After the session with Denny, my friend said in ten minutes time, she felt more understood than she had ever felt in her entire life. She is doing beautifully today and makes me so happy when I hear from her.

Even a dog bite can be used as a gift from the Divine!

I continue to love Osi, giving him ghee every day, giving him my undivided attention in the morning and in the evening, and giving him unconditional love.

"Whatever you do in life, give your 100 percent."

Dr. Pankaj Naram

From *Ancient Secrets of a Master Healer*, p. 75

Lisa Lowe - Dr. Naram to the Rescue

How I met Dr. Naram: I was doing a Google search for a health topic. I was looking into questions just for females, so I wanted to do some research on it and his name popped up. I watched some of his videos on YouTube about menopause and how some women were actually going out of menopause and getting pregnant. I thought that was fascinating. I always thought that could be true. I heard it through some other people that were able to reverse menopause, but here is this man on YouTube promoting that! I looked him up and went to his website and saw that he was going to be in Los Angeles (California) in two weeks, so I immediately set an appointment and took myself, my mom, and my daughter. I felt so good when I first met him, even though I was only with him for 10 minutes.

Just the fact that Dr. Naram asked me what I wanted really helped: that a stranger would just get me. But I wasn't coming to him in this helpless person stage. He presented to me like I mattered and was valued, and that I was heard and seen. He could also see people's longing and suffering. He asked me what I wanted, and I told him; I also told him about my animals. He seemed very excited, and I think when strangers act that way toward you, it lights something in you, and I think he knew. He knows that he knows. He knows what to do.

So, I became hooked and wanted to know more.

I knew he was coming back again shortly. I booked again and then brought my mom, my daughter, and my son-in-law. Everyone went. I sent as many people as I could. I brought my family. I was so interested in what Dr. Naram was offering.

I met Dr. Clint as well, and I was interested in knowing all this information that I was bugging them to teach!

Are you going to teach? Are you going to teach?

They said they're putting a school together in Germany and I immediately signed up even though I didn't really have all the funds, but I found a way to get there and make it happen.

It was very exciting, even though I was going through some challenging times.

Another time Dr. Naram came to LA: I rescued some baby mice, and I brought a little mouse with me to my appointment. He thought it was endearing. I had been in the rescue business since 2010; animal rescue, mainly dogs, but cats and horses as well as every living creature that needed a little help. I always was aiding creatures that needed help.

I also brought my four dogs. One had severe back issues, one had seizures and a heart issue, another one had a heart issue, and the fourth one had some other bone structure issues.

Dr. Naram was really busy. We stayed until like 3:00 a.m. in the morning and he worked on my dogs in front of everyone. Everyone was staying late. He read their pulses. He did adjustments and Marmaas on them. He gave me a formula for each one of them and each one of them included the detox tabs. When I take them, I get cramps in my intestines. I evacuate pretty quickly. Once your body gets used to it, you don't get that kind of feeling. But I thought, wow, giving that to my dogs, but it's to remove toxins, acids, and the Aam build up.

I gave the herbs and the detox to all of them. My heart dog named Corbin had a life expectancy of less than a year, and yet he lived another six years, so that's pretty good for his situation; so he lived to an average dog age.

My dog with the back issues and other problems, too, but he detoxed, and he actually lived longer than a large dog should, especially with back issues, but we just stuck with the fresh foods, the detox formulas, and the other herbs that were for their issues.

We did all that with my seizure dog as well and his prescribed herbs and detox formula was super important. He had seizures occasionally, but not like he would get them all the time. That was a great relief.

All the dogs definitely improved. I probably could have even taken it further.

At that time in my life, my own life was very congested with emotions and some family traumas, and so all those things that are happening at once get addressed and sometimes when you're healing more things come up to heal.

For me, one of my main goals in my own world is to just be in a very pristine, clean, self-contained environment with myself and whatever animal beings are present around me. Dr. Naram's treatments improved the quality and quantity of time of my dogs' lives, and I do actually think they could have lived even longer if I had advanced my situation a bit faster. But, you know, we were all in it, and we're all in life and we go with the best we can, where we are. And so I'm grateful for that.

That my dogs' lives got extended and were happier, felt better, and had more joy is the most important thing. It's about quality! Quality of life, and feeling good.

Esther Wolkowitz and Mamacita

A little knowledge, and the ability to trust where you are in the process of learning, can create miracles.

During the Immersion Course, we were tasked with listening to a recording of Dr. Naram in which one of the home remedies he described was for helping a person who was experiencing bloat. Within a couple of weeks, I was visiting a friend at his ranch. I adore all the animals at the ranch.

When I went out to see the goats and sheep my friend told me that one of his ewes, who was pregnant at the time, seemed to be experiencing bloat. This can be deadly for the sheep. She had been standing and not moving about for about 24 hours, without eating or drinking. I immediately thought of Dr. Naram's recording and his remedy for bloating. I decided that I had nothing to lose and that I was going to do my best to help this ewe, who I affectionately called Mamacita.

I went into the house and found the recording of Dr. Naram. I gathered as many of the ingredients from the kitchen and improvised on the amounts necessary. Mamacita does not have a belly button to apply the remedy and she is a lot larger than a human. I did not measure any of the ingredients. I made about a cup of paste with what I had available. For example, I did not have Asafetida. I juiced an onion and garlic and added turmeric.

Lesson Learned:

- Document all remedies and improvised recipes!

I massaged the paste onto Mamacita's belly for about 20 minutes, rubbing in a circular motion. She did not move or try to get away. My friend, a disbeliever, said "well, either it will do something, or she will be dead in the morning anyway."

After the massage we stood and watched Mamacita. For the first time in a day, she laid down! I brought her a bowl of water and she took a couple of sips. Something had changed. As it was nighttime, we left her and went into the house. For me it was an anxious night.

At first light we went out to the pen and found that Mamacita had moved and was now standing by the water trough. Her son, from a pregnancy a year prior, was by her side. As we stood and watched, her son started for the corral. Mamacita followed! I felt I was witnessing a miracle. Somehow, I was able to help. Mamacita went on to deliver her baby three weeks later.

Lessons Learned:

- Make an electronic file of remedies on your phone

- Don't be afraid to try something new on animals

- Don't be afraid to use and trust your intuition to make an adjustment or change to the remedies when you don't have the exact ingredients. (Think of the properties and purposes of each spice as learned during the course.)

- Be prepared for miracles!

- Don't be discouraged if something does not work. It is a learning process.

- Onions and garlic are okay as a massage paste but should not be given in food to most domestic animals.

"When you have a burning desire, with faith, commitment, and discipline, then anything is possible."

Baba Ramdas, Dr. Naram's Master

From *Ancient Secrets of a Master Healer,* p. 160

Jayna Taylor and Oakley

"He is such a GOOOD boy!" his new groomer, authentically assured me. "He's so full of life! I would've never guessed that his age was 14."
I nodded my head in agreement as my heart knew this is true. This is generally what I hear when people meet Oakley. He is a happy, bouncing bundle of fur who carries around a plush toy in his mouth when he is happy!

Oakley was born in March of 2009. He is a rare-black, ShihTzu-Maltese poodle. My daughter adopted him with the hopes he would be the size of a purse dog. She had dreams of carrying him around as her companion everywhere she went. Oakley outgrew the size of a purse as he has more of the ShihTzu body - 15 lbs.

Oakley's home as a puppy was active as he had two older dog brothers, boxers. Charley and Boomer were tall, 5 times the height of Oakley. They were big and gentle.

The three of them were great friends! Regularly Oakley would be playing and would get under their long legs and get stepped on by accident. He was so much smaller than the others.

Charlie transitioned to the dog park in the sky. A new Boxer dog, Diesel, joined the family. Two years later Boomer transitioned to the dog park in the sky and another boxer puppy, Harley, joined the household.

The two boxers were young, but big puppies. The dogs were all fighting for attention and alpha position. With a newborn baby in the household, there was too much going on. Oakley was becoming more stressed, anxious, and defensive. At age 6, Oakley came to live with me, Nana!

The year was 2014. Oakley adjusted rather quickly to being the center of attention and rewarded often. Oakley has the most adorable skip in his step. He was injured when he was a pup as he was under foot, unknowingly. I was concerned that arthritis would set in that leg as he got older.

At age 10, Oakley and I moved to the state of California for 5 months. I watched Oakley's begin to diminish. Separation anxiety was beginning, and he was territorial. He would bark at noises and people walking by.

In August 2017, we did a big move across the country to the state of Georgia which is a 3-day journey. The separation anxiety got worse. He had to be in my lap or by my side. It was a big change, and it was hard on him.

He gained weight, he was mopey, which made it hard for him to get around. He was fearful and he was in pain. He was licking and chewing his paws. He was doing his best to be in his body.

Fleas and ticks are in abundance in that area. I noticed that he was lethargic. His scratching was excessive. He was battling fleas and he picked up ticks. He shut down until I found the tick and got it out of his body. He was limping more, strange bumps appeared on his body. His body was tender when I touched him. I was worried! As a pet mom, I was concerned about tapeworms, Lyme disease, arthritis, and cancer.

In 2019, I was working with Ayushakti's Dr. Ronak. I shared these concerns with him. Sent photos of the growths and he gave me some herbs that he thought would help!

Ayushakti Herbs – for Oakley

- *Skintonic* – for healthy skin
- *Granthihar* – Pitta balance, for muscles and tissues
- *Kaishore Guggul* – Healthy Skin
- *Ayurcid* – Digestion
- *Painmukti M.J.* – Supports healthy bones and joints
- *Painmukti Sandhical* – for healthy bones, hair, and nails
- *Rasnadi Guggul* – for minor pain

- *Virofight* – Immune system and respiratory support
- *Immuno* – Immunity booster

Diet to include moong beans & veggies

Within 30 days I saw improvement! He was getting around much better, the weight was coming off, I could tell he didn't have as much pain. The bumps disappeared. He could walk further and further every day.

He was getting his hop back, his happiness back, he started to carry his toy around in his mouth again. He stopped licking his paws, and he stopped scratching so much.

I stopped giving him the Ayushakti formulas and the symptoms all came back. I gave Oakley the formulas and the symptoms all went away.

When Dr. Hemang came to Atlanta, he did a pulse reading on Oakley. He said that over Zoom and photos, Dr. Ronak had the perfect recommendation! He didn't change a thing; it was just perfect.

Oakley is still on most of the supplements. He is a good boy! It's hard to believe that he is 14 years young!

Jody Curtis: Tiki, Ricky, & Moong Bean Soup

Lots of LOVE!

When I began learning the Ancient Secrets and enjoying the moong bean soup, I started feeling more and more centered and peaceful. I had a sore on my ankle that I had for several years that wasn't healing, and after one week on the soup and herbs it just vanished completely, never to return. My joints feel better, and the inflammation went away in my body. The moong bean soup has become a staple in my diet, and I have eaten it several times a week for the last 2 ½ years and so have my two small dogs!

My dogs have both experienced healing from eating the moong bean soup with the vegetables, herbs and ghee and they both LOVE it!

Both dogs were adopted and have pretty severe trauma from past abuse. Tiki (our chiweenie), had a golf ball size lump in her throat that we just thought was her "Adams apple." It didn't seem to bother her, and she really loved us to rub on her throat and she would lean into it. Only a couple weeks and a few cups of soup later, my daughter and I both noticed that Tiki just seemed happier. When I was petting her throat, I noticed that the lump was completely gone!

Ricky, the older dog had very dark eyes and after eating the soup his eyes have also lightened up to a brown color from black and become more sparkly. He has arthritis in his back hip, and he seems like he feels much better when he's eating the moong bean soup...he's more active and happier.

They are both small dogs, so I usually only feed them a little (¼ to ½ cup) a few times a week and their coats are so shiny now! They are acting more playful too! The moong bean soup has lots of vegetables (no garlic or onions), herbs, and ghee (good fats) in it, so it removes inflammation in both animals and humans.

Our dogs go crazy when it is their time to get their soup! We even taught Tiki, our chiweenie, to say mooooong! I usually mix it with a little chicken or their regular dry (grain-free) dog food. Use your intuition for feeding your animals and see the amazing results!

Punam Patel: Reiki and Luna

As a Reiki Master, I have worked with many different animals over the years. Energy healing has been one of the greatest ancient secrets that is very powerful and easily accessible to all.

Reiki is the universal life force, also known as energy; it has many names, prana, chi, ki and light, just to name a few.

We are all born with this universal life force in us. We are born as a perfectly tuned symphony orchestra. Babies and children are the best examples of this life force, as it flows through them fully, they are able to stay in the space of love and joy. You'll see, even when they get hurt or are triggered by something, unlike adults, they are able to snap out of it very quickly and return back to their original state of love and joy. We've all seen a child go from crying to suddenly smiling and laughing, within seconds.

Over time, due to our programming and conditioning, our perfectly tuned symphony orchestra becomes 'out of tune'. As stagnant energy enters our bodies, our chakras get blocked. As our chakras stop spinning, so does Universal Energy, therefore, we no longer flow in harmony with nature, causing stress and anxiety. This also happens to animals. They too, are born with this universal life force and as stagnant energy enters, they also become blocked, leading to the cause of disease, illness, and stagnation.

As a Reiki Master, I have the ability to tap into the energetic field of both humans and animals. With animals, this has allowed me to communicate with them, ask them what they are experiencing, or simply be able to relay messages back to them and let them know they are safe and loved. I have been able to uncover the cause of whatever discomfort they are in and most importantly put the universal energy back into their bodies, which then pushes the stagnant energy out and starts spinning their chakras again. When they are flowing in harmony with nature, disease can no longer enter their field.

I truly believe we all have the ability to channel healing energy into our animals. The universal life force lives within us, it is what we are made of. Even when stagnant, it is still inside us, waiting patiently, like a sleeping snake, waiting to uncoil and rise to our commands. How? Well, energy flows where attention goes. Yes, it is that simple, place your attention to wherever you want this universal life force to go within your pet, and imagine it, as a beautiful white light, as shiny and bright as a full moon. Then, think of a moment where you experienced blissful love. You'll feel your entire vibration change as you tune into it. Now you've opened the channel to flow this energy from you to your pet.

My Alaskan Klee Kai, Luna, suffers from anxiety, just like many other pets do. I've been channeling reiki energy into her for years. I find it helps calm her and relieve her anxiousness and unease.

I have worked with many animals, from dogs that were acting out and being vicious, to horses suffering from severe pain to many sick animals suffering from various diseases. One thing they've all had in common is their pure love for their human parent. When ill and on their last days, their worry about leaving their parent behind outweighed their pain and even fear of dying. It is one of the most loving and purest things I've been honored to witness.

Your love for your pet is the gateway to their healing. Through that love flows the universal energy through you right into them. Take your attention to wherever they may need the healing, hold your hands out, hovering above the spot where it is needed, then visualize that beautiful white light and let it flow through you. Keep your attention on the spot where you want the energy to go.

Remember, energy flows to where your attention goes. Think of pure thoughts of love: this will strengthen the channel and raise the vibration of your pet to the highest frequency of love and light. There is no greater healing than love.

---Punam Patel: Advanced Hypnosis & Hypnotherapy, Reiki, and Regression | Los Angeles, CA

http://punampatelhypnotherapy.com

punam@Punampatelhypnotherapy.com

Dr. Stephen Wechsler & Hank

Dr. Stephen Wechsler: drsteveradio@gmail.com

Social time is important for animals as well as people! Fresh air and sunshine are the best remedies.

Dr. Stephen Wechsler

Vinay Soni and Dr. Naram Pet Stories

Dr. Naram Saving a Husky

This is a story that happened around 2004 or 2005 and is about Dr. Naram and a husky dog. One day the owner of the Dog Rescue Foundation came into Dr. Naram's office. He said to Dr. Naram, "I have brought one very sick dog. Can you check him?"

So he brought the Husky dog into the Malad clinic at Ayushakti. He opened a blanket to show the doctor, and when we saw it, we really felt sorry for that dog, because it was so dangerously underweight. We could easily see his ribs. He was trying to reach his back to scratch his dry, inflamed skin, but he was not able to do it: he was too weak. He was also shivering.

Dr. Naram checked the dog and said that he had parasites, a bacterial infection, and lots of skin issues on his back, as well as low immunity.

Slowly Dr. Naram started his treatment, applying the Sudarun Lotion and Sepnil Cream, and, of course, Skin Tonic Cream. He gave remedies like Suniram, Immuno, Skin Tonic, Kaishore Guggul, and Virechan. Because he had a lot of heat in the body, he was shaking/vibrating to pass the motion to remove the toxins.

As for his food, Dr. Naram said to give him a home remedy: 1 tsp. ghee mixed with ¼ tsp. black pepper powder. He also recommended giving additional ghee in the food and more turmeric powder, as that would internally help heal the skin situation.

After a year and a few months, the dog grew new, full hair like a healthy dog. And it was the first time I came to know how a husky dog SHOULD look and we really enjoyed seeing his healing progress.

This story was transformational for me. I was so moved by the way Dr. Naram loved the animal. When we saw that husky dog for the first time, we felt like he may die anytime. He was so boney and so weak that he could not reach his back. He was shivering so much because of the low immunity. But now all of that is in the past, thanks to these ancient secrets and Dr. Naram.

Dr. Naram and a Dog Named Sheru

In the early days of his practice, Dr. Naram saw a dog we will call Sheru. This dog was having painful arthritis, so he was not moving at all and if somebody came near him, because of his pain and the arthritis, he would bark loudly and disrupt people around him.

Dr. Naram approached Sheru very slowly and lovingly, and did a Marmaa and checked the pulse. He found out that Sheru had severe, painful arthritis in his joints, which is why he was barking.

Dr. Naram started treatment for him by giving him Sandhiyog, Painmukti M.J., and Painmukti Sandhical. The supplements and changes in the diet made a big difference. Dr. Naram advised Sheru's owners to give ghee with turmeric, and one meal with moong beans or Kitchari. They gave him ground sesame seeds for natural calcium so that his joints and bones would become stronger. All these things combined so that that dog got rid of the arthritis pain and stiffness.

Dr. Naram and the Kitty Who Couldn't Go

This kitty named Daisy was having lots of gas issues and an uncomfortable stomach situation. Because of that, Daisy used to bite everyone and anyone who came near her. Dr. Naram, as usual, approached Daisy with so much love! He did the Marmaa so slowly that the kitty became calm and cool. Dr. Naram discovered that she was constipated and bloated. That's why this cat was behaving so badly!

Dr. Naram gave Daisy Amrutas, Anulom, Gasmukti, and Blis. Also for constipation, Amrutadi Churna to help pass the motions and very slowly, Daisy released all the constipation and was free from the bloating and discomfort. Daisy was still living a healthy life when I last saw the cat in 2018.

She was so lovable. And with her improved health, the quality of her hair also improved because Dr. Naram said when you have a high Vata situation, it affects the hair of the animals just like it does with people.

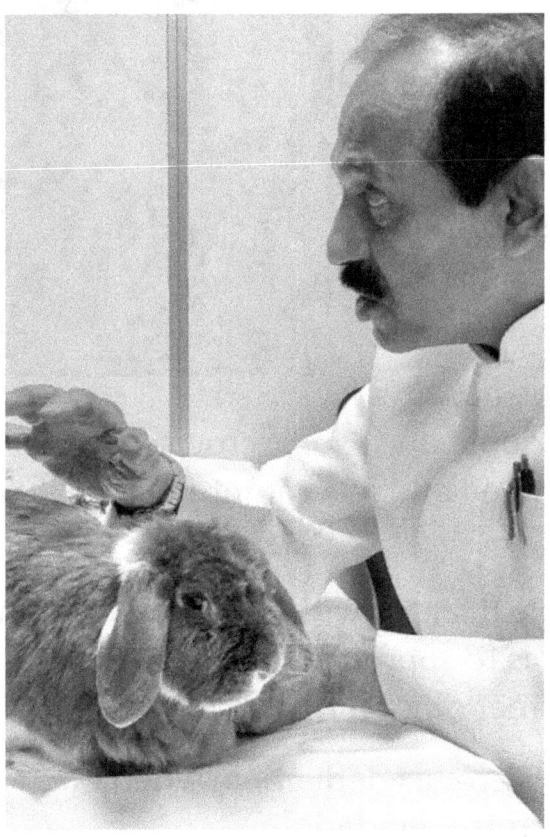

Dr. Pankaj Naram, reading the pulse of a rabbit

Mirayah & Street Dogs in India

During our *Miracle Experience Experiment* course, we were encouraged to welcome the unexpected guest as if the Divine has come to visit or sent a lesson for us to learn.

Part of the activity was to seek out cows, dogs, crows, or other animals that are in need and feed or interact in kindness with them.

For people in areas without access to animals, one option is to support Mirayah as she feeds and cares for street dogs in Mumbai.

Donations are tax deductible when made through Ancient Secrets Foundation:

www.AncientSecretsFoundation.org/product/atithi-devo-bhava-donation/

Mike and the Pashupatinath Dogs of Nepal

In April 2023, Dr. Clint G. Rogers and about 15 others in his Nepal Tour Group visited the Pashupatinath Ashram where several hundred street dogs have been rescued and are fed and cared for by the Aghori and Naths.

Their food is made from rice, fresh vegetables, and chicken. It's made fresh daily, and the dogs have to wait for it to cool off before they can eat it.

The dogs showed remarkable constraint as they patiently waited for the command from Mike that the food was cool enough to eat.

Dog Psalms: I Forgive

I am Dog. I forgive without asking for forgiveness.

I will forgive before you are ready to receive my look, my lick on your hand. I do not bargain forgiveness; I do not make a deal. You are forgiven even before you harm or holler or neglect or ignore. Tomorrow is a new day. Tonight is already a new time. The sun will not set on my anger. I forgive you and I am yours and you are mine. We agreed without a signed document. You can hold my words I cannot say, to a sentence I cannot write. Hold me to who I am. I am Dog and I forgive. Forgiving feels right. I do not ask why. I will not sleep with a grudge.

Herbert Brokering, author of Dog Psalms
www.augsburgbooks.com

Ancient Secrets & Horses

Peggy Coleman Taylor: We Owe so Much to Horses

The horse is the largest native herbivore in North America and is recorded to date having survived over 50 million years. More than 300 horse breeds are in the world today. Horses have been used for centuries for transportation, farming, even delivering mail via the Pony Express. We owe so much to the horse in the development of our nation, especially in the West.

The horse is often called nature's farmers. Thanks to their monogastric stomachs, they do not chew up the seeds from the native grasses they eat so when pooping, the seeds come out whole, which means they are replanting naturally, just like the elephants.

Whether the horse is wild, domestic, large, or small, when they sense danger they run away as fast as possible by nature's design.

Unfortunately, many horses are confined to fenced areas and if threatened they may stand to defend their safety. We should all respect the boundaries that each individual horse may require and whenever approaching a horse you are not familiar with, first ask permission from the owner.

Horses are very family oriented, and we can learn so much by just sitting and observing them. Observe the ears on a horse; if they are held stiff with the ear openings pointed forward, that indicates alertness and concentration. If the horse's ears are flat and pinned back, the horse might be telling you it's irritated or feeling territorial.

    The wild horses' priority is family, safety, and food. Horses are renowned for being able to help people heal. It is said horses mirror your soul. Consider yourself lucky whenever you are in the company of these centennial beings.

Ann Wilkinson's Horse Stories

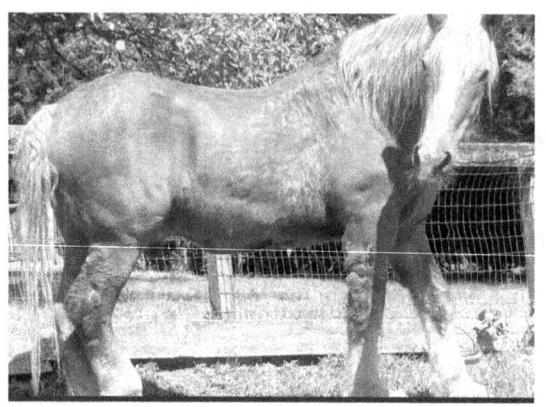

Mickey was an amazing therapeutic riding horse. One time I had a group of kids come from Philadelphia that were severely handicapped, and they were super late. None of their teachers who came with them were familiar with animals because they were all from the big city. These were big kids, around 19 years of age and older.

Because they were so late arriving, my family got tired of waiting. Everybody took off and did their own thing and left me alone. Mickey had to put 12 people on him that were very severely handicapped and large boned. It was a lot to ask of any horse, let alone an aging one!

Even though it was getting dark, I was bound and determined that every kid was going to get his or her turn to ride on this horse. Mickey put his front foot out and down for each one of them to get on. I didn't even know he knew how to do that. It was one of the most phenomenal experiences of my life. I'm so glad I didn't cancel it just because they were late.

One young man in this school group knew all kinds of amazing facts. When he left, he said, "Can I come here and live with you? You can adopt me, and I could help you with all your chores!"

I've cried about it for years.

Mickey started to lay down in the field and was not able to get up and when we would help him get up, all his bones would make cracking noises and I really had to consider if it was time to put him out of his misery. When he took even one step, all of his bones would snap like thick twigs, maybe 10 to 20 times with each step. I was in the middle of the Ancient Secrets 100-Day course, and I was thinking, well, if this were a human I would give them oil. What kind of oil can I use for a horse? The next time I went to the feed store it just so happened they were making a blend for dogs and horses. She supplied me with a combination oil of sunflower, omega-3, and other plant combinations.

I started giving him about a half a cup a day and his cracking rapidly reduced to zero. He lived another couple of years, and I was even able to get on his back and bareback ride him very gently up until a week before he died at the age of 31. I feel so good that I was able to give him relief, and that the last couple of years of his life were so pleasant. His bones went from brittle and cracking to springy and lubricated. I am so grateful.

Joy: Paint Quarter Horse

I had another amazing experience with my animals and the remedies. I have an old beautiful rescue paint horse named Joy, and she started to lay down a lot. I thought maybe it was her heart and then I noticed that her feet were tender when the ground got hard. When the farrier (someone who specializes in care of hoofs) came, he said he felt she had something called laminitis.

No matter who you talk to you in the horse world, when you mention laminitis, they say put your horse down (meaning euthanize your animal). It's the beginning of the end; it's terribly painful. The consensus is that nothing can help a horse with *laminitis.*

I gave her homeopathic belladonna and I put homeopathic Traumeel cream on her feet and I noticed that she was laying down a little bit less and she was coming closer to her feeding area. One day however, I got the impulse to put turmeric in her food. I looked it up and it was safe for horses, and from the very first time that I put it in her food, she came for her food enthusiastic and nickering! She comes right up to the feed stand requesting her food! I have not seen her laying down. I am on day six or seven of the turmeric and she's up early every morning and asking for her food now that it has turmeric in it. She ravages her food!

I added oil to her food some time ago and I doubled the amount of sunflower, safflower, and omega 3 oil. Now I use only the oil and turmeric and she is so much happier.

Homeopathy and Ayurveda has brought so much hope and fearlessness to my life. I cry when I think of the unnecessary suffering when sometimes the remedy is so very simple.

Remedy: I give her about a tablespoon of turmeric powder daily, but I started with a teaspoon and worked my way up. Additionally, I give her about ½- ¾ cup oil, 2 times a day.

Update: It's over a year later and she is still happy and standing and if she has a flareup, we use an acute remedy. We still get to have JOY in our lives and did not have to put her down.

She's very, very sweet and does very well with little children.

Heidi Aden and Santana

Horse healing places offering equine therapy are popular and have a proven track record for helping with physical and emotional issues, especially in children.

When I was younger, I had a few major surgeries. When I was 12 years old, I was lucky to get a horse of my own, even though it was only on 'lease' for a few years through the 4-H program.

I know taking care of him helped me through a lot of frustration and gave me purpose and a new outlook just from taking care of him. I also won some trophies and ribbons in horse shows.

I wrote for advertisers that did equine therapy in the magazine that my mom and I used to publish in the 80's and 90's.

- Heidi Aden, Lion's Pen Graphics
  LionsPenGraphics.com

Ayurveda & Horses

In Ayurveda, a Dosha refers to fundamental energy. Ashwa Ayurveda explains the Doshas for horses:

- Vata horses are extremely outgoing, lean, and vibrant.
- Pitta horses are competitive, athletic type. It can physically carry you for miles.
- Kapha horses are the big, beautiful horses on the heavier side. They are calm and compassionate.

Shalihotra Samhita details the nature and varieties of horses, description of various diseases like fever, colic, diarrhea, and fractures. It also explains about the benefits of herbs for horses such as Triphala, Guggulu, Haritaki, Laksha, etc.

Ashwagandha root is an excellent addition to your horse's menu! It's an adaptogenic herb, an overall health tonic that can support the immune system, strengthen muscle tone, and can rejuvenate the horse's body and mind to restore health. Ashwagandha's function is to provide protection to the nervous system. Its vital role as an anti-depressant/anti-anxiety herb has garnered accolades in the medical field. Studies have proven this powerful herb provides the same effects as prescription anti-anxiety drugs such as Ativan.

Ashwagandha powder can easily be added to your horse's or pet's meals.[1] The recommended serving is about ⅛ teaspoon daily for every 20 pounds. You'll have to do the math for a horse! Or better yet, check with a vet that specializes in natural health for horses.

Shankhpushpi, an Indian herb, is another Ayurvedic favorite. It has a synergestic effect when combined with Ashwagandha root; herbs can be much more powerful in specific combinations.[2]

Shankhpushpi herb is excellent for treating panic attacks, sleep disorders, and varying degrees of nervousness. It is a fantastic calming herb for the traveling horse.

---

[1] 5 Ayurvedic Herbs You Can Use to Support Your Pet's Health and Well-Being

[2] Balance your horse with these ayurvedic herbs

Ancient Secrets and Birds

Carol K. Ray: Birds, Vultures, and Energy

- *Carol Ray*

I saw a video on Facebook a few years ago that showed using birds of prey as teachers of energy management. This is my story of using the ancient secret of Atithi Devo Bhava (P. 286 in ASMH), treating any unexpected guest (birds, cows, dogs, emotions, people, interruptions, whatever) as if God has come to bring you a gift or lesson.

The Miracle of Vultures

I would not hesitate to help a crow - they are smart and can be loyal. But I hate black vultures! Turkey vultures are fine with me, but black vultures in central Texas have become predatory and can exhibit well organized brutality! They watch for cows giving birth and... I will spare you the gory details, but it's been witnessed repeatedly since about 2004! The cost for lost stock has been ranging from $15,000 to $20,000 a year for some Texas ranchers. Black vultures were protected by law in Texas until 2022.

I have had 3 on my farm that harassed my dog on a regular basis. They roost together on my old barn. They have been coming here for years. Yesterday I was chasing them away, yelling at them, being tired of the dog barking at them and I noticed only two. They left my rooftop and went to an abandoned shed that sits next to my property line; they were working on a hole in the roof, making it bigger! That seemed odd. At sunset I noticed something inside and it was big, and I saw what looked like white wings hit the window.

As I started to look closer to see what it was, I heard, then saw, a swarm of bees. These bees have twice been Africanized- and have been extremely aggressive so I conquered my curiosity and let the trapped black vulture be.

The next day I was outside and heard another crash into a window at the abandoned shed. In the 14 years I have lived on my farm, I have never trespassed on that old, abandoned building. But I looked in the window and saw one of the big ugly black vultures in there! I thought about the "miracle game" and assignment with dogs, cows and crows; and remembered what Dr. Clint Rogers said about seeing a rat in his apartment that it could be considered a gift to get in touch with a persisting fear or other emotion.... I didn't want this big ugly nasty bird to die of dehydration or starvation if I could save it.

It took all the courage I could muster to force that old, rotten door open. Slowly I went inside, and we saw each other and SCARED each other about the same time! I squealed like a little schoolgirl! I left the door open as I ran out of it, and eventually the vulture managed to come out and fly away.

How smart are they that its buddies were trying to make it an escape hatch on the roof? Going inside this old building was a huge leap of faith! I have been prideful about never trespassing and yet I did it to save something I truly despise; but vultures are God's creatures, too, and it was the loving thing to do!

Vulture Saga Continues

I live in a barn (with a barndamenium on top) I had built in 2010, after a tornado destroyed the old barn. It has a steep pitch on the roof, and dormers above the windows. Birds have chewed and clawed into the wood and are living in the kitchen dormer. I pound on the ceiling, my dog Osi barks, and I leave Zumba music playing loudly when I leave to try and discourage them, but they persist.

Adding even more sleep disruption, squirrels have, in the past few days, chewed through the peak of the roof near my bedroom and are nesting in the wall! It drives me (and Osi) crazy!

Yesterday, I was outside taking a break from work, and heard a squirrel barking. He was at my roof peak looking down at the ground, pounding his tail, sounding an alarm. This went on for over a half hour. My best guess is that it was a snake sunning itself in our 80-degree weather. I mentally thanked the squirrel for the alarm and mentally asked that they relocate to one of the nearby trees and leave the barn so I can sleep!

I saw one of the Black Vultures on top of our old garage; maybe the one I rescued. Osi was telling him to get off our property. I watched as it swooped down near the barn and picked something up; it was at a distance but looked like a snake or maybe a rat tail. Maybe it was ridding the farm of dangerous rattlesnakes or a nasty rat. Maybe it was repaying me for saving it.

Atithi Devo Bhava Part 2:

It happened again! On the Ancient Secrets Global Healing Call 26 April 2020, and after some explosive family drama during the breakout room chats, I went outside and again saw a large bird smacking the glass in the windows of an abandoned farm building next door to my property in Texas. I guessed correctly that it was again a vulture trapped and once again my resolve was being tested to walk through the rattlesnake infested grass and see if I could coax it out of the building to its freedom.

Regardless of how I felt about the behavior of the black vulture, it became clear that this was something I had to do: conquer my fear, ego, and prejudice, and rescue this black vulture from its misfortune; I had to see the Divine in it.

Believe it or not, after the second rescue as seen in the video (https://youtu.be/EuAQHzXZrhY), the committee of vultures moved to the peak of my barn and in the process, the squirrels and nesting birds moved out of my barn attic! I can sleep peacefully once again!

Carol Ray
June 2020

Update: Summer 2022

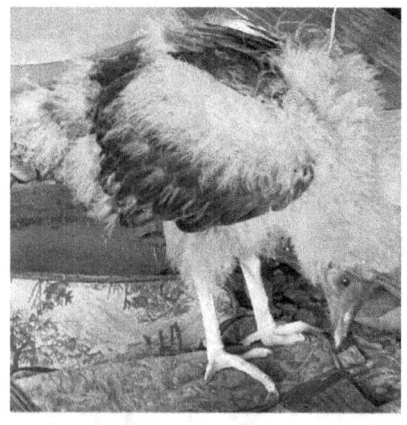

The vultures put a baby in my carport for safe keeping while it was getting its adult, black features. It resembled a big yellow chicken! I named it Baby Big Bird ("BBB") and for whatever reason, decided to sing a mantra to it, every day when encountering it:

Om Namo, Bhagavate, Vasudevaya.

BBB decorated its nest with Christmas ornaments it dug out of boxes in my carport! Red and gold ornaments, a stocking, a stuffed Christmas hedgehog, and some garland. It was lovely! I watched as it was fed daily by its parents and saw it venturing out into the open (vultures have little defense mechanisms other than expelling bile from their gullet to the attacker). I was witness to BBB's initial flight to the top of the abandoned building. BBB came to visit often on my deck at my barndamenium, usually with several friends, including a youngster with a few yellow feathers.

Living with vultures has taught me many things. I have learned how to calm myself and center my energy. I do this before approaching them. Now I can see them as part of the great circle of life that we are all connected to, and to admire their creativity!

Baby Big Bird with only a few yellow feathers on his head, showing his beautiful wings to scare off offending swallows.

Dr. Giovanni Brincivalli & the Eagle

Dr. Pankaj Naram and I were walking on the street in India and we saw this eagle on the other side of the street; it was not moving, not trying to fly, not trying to escape. It appeared very weak. On close inspection, we could not see any injury: no blood, no apparent wounds of any kind. I found a cardboard box and carefully put the eagle in the box and took it back to my room.

The next day we were traveling to Mumbai. We were feeding the eagle and began giving it Ayushakti's Jivanyog, a natural immune booster which also give strength to the heart and improve the eagle's circulation.

Slowly the eagle began to get stronger and after some time regained full power. It was a big joy in the moment we could free this eagle and it could return to the skies.

Dr. Clint in front of the Milan Cathedral
(Duomo di Milano), Italy

"Everything can either be a poison or a medicine, depending on how you use it..."

Master Jivaka (Physician to the Buddha)

From *Ancient Secrets of a Master Healer,* p. 55

Emergencies & Pets

Our pets and animals are dependent on us to help them survive when disasters strike.

Don't let your animals down.

The time to plan is now!

Accidents happen, and when a pet faces a medical emergency, decision-making can be challenging, especially at night. It is crucial to have an emergency plan in advance. Discuss an emergency protocol with your vet, checking if they offer 24-hour service or work with an emergency clinic. Keep the clinic's details accessible.

Signs of a pet needing emergency care include pale gums, rapid breathing, weak pulse, temperature change, difficulty standing, paralysis, loss of consciousness, seizures, or excessive bleeding.

For severely injured pets, protect yourself first. Approach dogs calmly, call for help if aggressive, or use a makeshift stretcher for passive ones. For cats, cover their head to prevent biting and place them in a carrier.

Transport your pet to an emergency care facility once it is safe. Perform first aid, like elevating and applying pressure for bleeding or checking for choking. Perform CPR if needed, checking breathing and administering artificial respiration and chest compressions.

If your pet ingests something toxic, call your vet or the ASPCA Poison Control Center at (888) 426-4435 for guidance based on your pet's age, health, and ingested substance.

Essential Oils & Cats & Dogs

Rapid diagnosis and treatment are imperative. If you believe that your cat has ingested or come in contact with essential oils or liquid potpourri, call your veterinarian or Pet Poison Helpline (800-213-6680 (in USA)), a 24/7 animal poison control center, immediately. The sooner you seek treatment, the better the prognosis and outcome for your cat or dog.[3]

Cats: Bad for Cats & to be Avoided

Many liquid potpourri products and essential oils are poisonous to cats. Both ingestion and skin exposure can be toxic:

- Bay oil
- Bergamot oil
- Cinnamon oil
- Citrus oil
- Citronella oil
- Clove oil
- Eucalyptus oil
- Fir oil
- Geranium oil
- Grapefruit oil
- Juniper oil
- Lemon oil
- Lime oil
- Peppermint oil
- Pine oil
- Sweet birch oil
- Thyme oil
- Wintergreen oil
- Ylang-ylang oil

---

[3] Essential Oil and Liquid Potpourri Poisoning in Cats

The research on essential oils both in humans and pets is not concrete enough to definitely state that a cat will benefit from essential oils in a certain way. However, the experiences of other cat owners cannot be ignored.

Several Cat owners swear by essential oil to improve a cat's life. Some of the benefits of essential oils include:

- Flea repellent: The struggle against fleas on a cat can be a tough one. There are several products on the market to deal with this issue, but some cat owners are simply not comfortable exposing their cats to harsh chemicals. If you also prefer to minimize the number of chemicals in your cat's life, essential oils such as rosemary and cedarwood may just work for you.

- Improve mood: There's no denying how relaxing a mist of air from the diffuser filled with essential oils can be. Essential oils can have a similar effect on your cat. If used properly essential oils may have a positive effect on your cat's mood by reducing anxiety and depression

- Anti-inflammatory. Essential oils possess anti-inflammatory properties. This can be helpful if your cat suffers from inflammatory diseases or conditions like arthritis. It may also benefit simple inflammatory conditions like bruising.

According to the American Society for the Prevention of Cruelty to Animals (ASPCA) "in their concentrated form (100%), essential oils can absolutely be a danger for pets."

However, if used responsibly and in diluted forms, the following essential oils are considered safe[4]:

- Frankincense oil
- Cedarwood oil
- Helichrysum oil
- Rosemary oil
- Copaiba oil
- Roman or German oil
- Sweet pea oil
- Chamomile oil
- Lavender oil
- Valerian oil

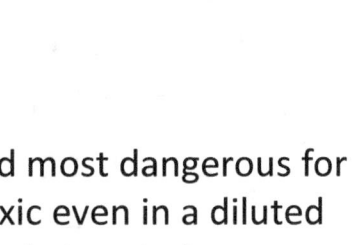

The essential oil considered most dangerous for cats is tea tree oil which is toxic even in a diluted form. Lavender is also very toxic to cats in a non-diluted form.

---

[4] Essential Oils for Cats: Benefits, Risks, & Considerations - Veterinarians.org

Use caution with dogs with these essential oils:

- Camphor
- Cassia
- Clove
- Mountain Savory
- Oregano
- Peppermint
- Thyme
- Wintergreen

"Every adversity - every difficult situation or heartbreak - has within it the seeds of equal or greater benefit."

Baba Ramdas, Dr. Naram's Master

From *Ancient Secrets of a Master Healer,* p. 29

Mindy Barrett: Evacuating with Pets – Lessons from the Lahaina Blaze

A lot of people are recognizing that the world can be more unpredictable than what we've been used to. Recently, unusual things seem to be happening more often. What we learned in the Lahaina Fire trying to evacuate with pets is that having a list of what your pets' needs are, in advance of the event, would be very useful.

It is not just what medications you need, although that is important. Grab cash, water, food. Important documents (deeds, birth certificates). Sentimental items like photo books or invaluable keepsakes come to mind. So many things race through your mind when faced with the loss and destruction of all that you own!

In addition to your important belongings, you need to grab your pet stuff as well. And just remember that even though you think you might be coming back later that day or the next day, that might not happen at all. If that's the case having cages or some kind of containment device, a carrier, a kennel, an airplane carrier, or anything like that is so helpful. My daughter, Madeline, was trying to corral 6 different animals, indoor and outdoor, technically ours, but really, the Communities, all at one time, because the fire was imminently approaching.

And it really worked well because she had some carriers. The ones that were skittish she was able to put in a carrier and the other ones she just said, "Get in the car," and off they went. When you're grabbing pets, when you're getting everybody together, just grab them. I mean, don't be super careful about not hurting anybody's feelings in those moments. Just get them in the car: put them in the pillowcases if that's what you have, just get them in the car. And because it's going to take them a long time to calm down anyway, an extra 30 seconds isn't going to matter. Getting straight into relative safety is more important.

She did not have time to grab food. She grabbed a couple bottles of water.

In hindsight, she would have liked to have had a bottle of water in the car all the time. Now granted, that's never really great, right? The plastic chemical leeches into the water and all that. You certainly don't want to make that your main water source, but in an emergency situation, having that kind of thing available in your car, can be life-saving.

They were stuck in the car for two days! With SIX ANIMALS! And had she not had a bottle of water it could have been really tragic because it was incredibly hot with limited gasoline and 6 animals in the car. It was a deeply uncomfortable scene.

The other thing that was helpful was that she did have small amounts of sedatives (Benadryl) for the pets so that in the moments when things were incredibly uncomfortable and discombobulating for them, she was able to give them some Benadryl just to take the edge off.

Another thing, when you're in the car, driving away, don't turn the radio on necessarily, or if you do turn it on, tune in to a soothing channel.

Remember too, once you get to a place that is seemingly safe, your pets are still really wound up and needing to decompress as well, and they may hide under the bed or the couch for a month! It's taken our pets months to really calm down and feel secure again.

Here is another little piece of advice: we immediately started trying to figure out how to get our pets off the island. Because housing was scarce and not everybody took pets, and we had six of them, I immediately started calling around to the pet transport places and inquired about what they were offering. I received a great deal of support right off the bat. The requests to get animals off the island really increased dramatically the following week, but I was on the phone with them like 2 days in and so I was actually the first person that they were talking to.

My advice would be ASK for what you need, just ask! And if they can't do it, they'll tell you, but just ask. And the same thing is true with Airbnb or hotels or any kind of lodging places. Lots of them say no pets, but in a situation like this, all rules are fluid. So just ask, just speak it out loud. Don't be afraid. The worst thing they're going to say is no, which is what you think it already is.

So that was really helpful because I just started asking for discounts. I asked for discounts from my vet. I asked for discounts from the airlines. I asked for discounts from Airbnb's. And every single place said yes. So I would encourage you to do that too. It is a way that you can advocate for yourselves and your pets in a financial way to facilitate everyone's safety.

Emergency Checklist for Evacuation

Some items you may want to include in an emergency Grab-and-Go bag for your pet: if you don't have pet carriers, consider purchasing a few laundry baskets big enough to house your pet, and include a container of zip ties and scissors. Put all the emergency supplies for your pets in the top basket that you can grab and go if needed. Then when you need a safe place for your pet, turn one basket on top of the other and zip tie them together for a make-shift cage. Here are some other ideas for evacuating in emergencies with your pets:

1. Food: Keep several days' supply of food, chew toys, and calming treats in an airtight, waterproof container.

2. Water: Store a water bowl and several days' supply of water.

3. Any medications your pet needs. Include a copy of their vaccination record.

4. First aid kit for pets: low dose Benadryl for allergies to new environments, better sleep, or nervous itching. The dose is 1 mg per pound, every 8 hrs. Dogs metabolize it differently than people do!

5. Calming herbal formulas. Flea treatments.

6. If space allows bring their cage or carrier for their protection. A comfy blanket or pillow and a few favorite toys can help. Other helpful items: Training pads. Muzzle.

7. Collar with ID tag and a harness or leash. Listing mobile phone numbers (instead of a landline/telephone number) and a secondary alternative number can be very helpful if your residence is no longer viable.

8. Do you have current photos of your pets and animals? It's an important part of rescuing them and getting them back if you get separated.

9. Signage: make it in advance - All People and Pets have been evacuated. OR We had no choice but to leave our pets behind: names, breed, where you last saw them.

10. Cats: Where cats hide- behind the refrigerator, under the bed and even inside the box spring, or under the sofa. Open a can of tuna and put it out while grabbing last minute items: sometimes that will bring them out of hiding.

11. Cats: If you don't have a cat carrier, use milk crates or laundry baskets. You can zip-tie them together as a make-shift crate. Using a pillowcase should be a last resort as they do not provide adequate ventilation in hot weather.

12. Do not chain dogs outside or lock them indoors. If you don't have ID tags, use a permanent marker to write your number in a visible spot. Write on a wide zip-tie and put around their neck.

13. Fish: always have a power backup for your aquarium. It doesn't take many hours of an outage to cause irreversible damage to aquariums.

PRACTICE! On the first day of the month, cut the power to your home and practice getting out safely, including with your pets.

For additional information:
Prepare Your Pets for Disaster
https://www.ready.gov/pets

IN CASE OF EMERGENCY PLEASE SAVE OUR PETS!

☐ OTHER: _____
_____

EMERGENCY #: _____

"To become a true healer requires inner development, not just technical knowledge."

Dr. Giovanni Brincivalli

From *Ancient Secrets of a Master Healer,* p. 190

Helping Your Pet To Heal

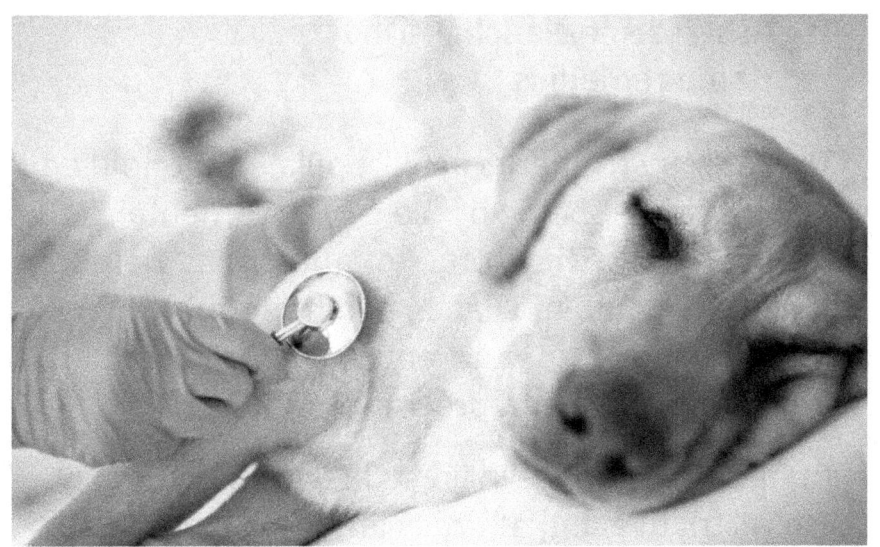

Six Instruments of Siddha-Veda

According to the philosophy and the ancient teachings of Siddha-Veda, there are six essential instruments necessary to achieve a lasting and vibrant health.[5] These include:

- Diet
- Lifestyle
- Herbal supplements
- Marmaa
- Ashtakarma/Panchakarma
- Home remedies

These six instruments act like pillars that hold and support the well-being of the physical, mental, and emotional body. This is true for animals as well. To create and maintain balance and harmony in our life and theirs, the ancient art and science of Siddha-Veda offers simple and precise guidelines.

At first the changes in lifestyle and the diet may seem restrictive and at times impossible to follow. But even small changes can have significant results although it does take time. Celebrate the wins of making positive small changes for you and your pets and use the rest as opportunities to do better tomorrow.

---

[5] Dr. Pankaj Naram: Healthy Diet Recommendations by Dr. Pankaj Naram

Pets and Siddha-Veda - Ayurveda

Dr. Naram loved animals and many videos are available with remarkable healing journeys for dogs, cats, tigers, elephants, alligators, and even bees! Veterinary Siddha-Veda/Ayurveda provides a benefit not only for the animal, but also for the pet guardian. For the animal, Ayurveda provides greater longevity and well-being, a preventative approach, and a deep regard for the innate self-healing power of animals.[6]

For the pet guardian, Siddha-Veda/Ayurveda provides a healthier, happier companion animal and a safer home environment, free from the hazards of cross-species communicable diseases such as giardiasis. Natural remedies and healthy approaches are also less expensive than either allopathy or supplements, a benefit for your pocketbook.

Not all pets will enjoy a little spa massage and oil for the pads on the paws. But it is an aspect of Panchakarma that some might love!

---

[6] Veterinary Ayurveda: Case Histories of Five Cats — Alandi Ayurveda

What are Doshas

Doshas are predominantly made of 5 elements: earth, water, fire, air, and space (ether). Siddha-Veda suggests that these Doshas, Vata, Pitta, and Kapha, are the primary qualities or principles that govern every human body and are present in animals and plants.

Ayurveda is an ancient system of holistic medicine that originated in India and has been used for thousands of years to treat various health conditions in humans and animals. Ayurveda is based on the concept of balancing the three Doshas (Vata, Pitta, and Kapha) that govern the body and mind.[7]

According to an article from IVC Journal, Ayurveda in veterinary medicine has traditionally focused on animal welfare, treatment therapies, management, and surgery. The article also describes the characteristics of each dosha in animals and how to determine the body type of your pet. Ayurvedic herbs and modalities can be used to treat many common problems in animals, such as arthritis, skin allergies, digestive issues, anxiety, and more.[8]

Please consult your veterinarian before making any changes to your pets' diet or giving them any supplements.

---

[7] [8] Ayurveda in Veterinary Medicine

If you want to read more about Ayurveda in veterinary medicine, you can check out the following sources:

- IVC Journal Homepage:[9] This is the website of the *Integrated Veterinary Care Journal*, which provides information on the latest trends and innovations in integrative veterinary care.

- Ayurvedic Veterinary Medicine: Principles and Practices:[10] This is a chapter from the book *Veterinary Herbal Medicine*, which explains the basic principles and practices of Ayurvedic medicine in animals, including diagnosis, treatment, prevention, and wellness.

---

[9] [10] Ayurveda in Veterinary Medicine | IVC Journal

Vata Dosha in Animals

Vata is associated with the elements of air and ether. It regulates all the movements and functions of the body and mind. Vata animals are usually agile, active, and adaptable, but they can also become anxious, restless, and erratic when out of balance.[11]

Vata animals are often seen darting, hopping, or flying around, displaying their quick and lively nature. They are also curious and intelligent, but they may forget things easily or lose interest quickly.

Some examples of Vata animals are:

- Birds, especially those that are small, fast, and vocal, such as sparrows, hummingbirds, and parrots.

- Rodents, such as squirrels, mice, and rabbits; all are quick, alert, and adaptable.

- Deer, antelopes, and gazelles, that are graceful, swift, and easily startled.

- Cats, especially those that are lean, curious, and independent, such as Siamese, Bengal, and Abyssinian.

---

[11] Ayurveda in Veterinary Medicine | IVC Journal

Vata animals need a balanced diet, a warm and comfortable environment, and regular routines to keep their Vata in harmony. They also benefit from gentle massage, calming music, and affectionate companionship.[12]

Vata animals are slender and small.
They may have flat chests and be quite tall.
They might also be short, or even average in height
but have no muscles in sight.

Vata animals are restless and quick.
They have variable appetites and energy to lick!
They are sensitive to cold and may get sick
When their Dosha is out of harmony or a bone to pick.

Vata animals are creative and curious.
They love to explore and play.
They are friendly and generous
But they need balance for their best day.

By Carol Ray & Bing A.I.

---

[12] Ayurveda For Animals (dogsnaturallymagazine.com)

If you are interested in learning more about Vata in animals, you can check out these links:

- Learning to See the Doshas in Nature: This article explains how to recognize the doshas in different aspects of nature, including animals, plants, seasons, and times of day.
https://www.banyanbotanicals.com/info/blog-the-banyan-insight/details/learning-to-see-the-doshas-in-everything/

- Ayurveda For Animals: This article provides an introduction to Ayurveda for animals, and how to identify and balance the Doshas in your pets.
https://www.dogsnaturallymagazine.com/ayurveda-for-animals/

Pitta Dosha in Animals

Pitta is one of the three Doshas or biological energies, in Ayurveda. Pitta is composed of fire and water elements. Pitta governs metabolism, digestion, intelligence, and courage. Animals that have a dominant Pitta Dosha tend to have the following traits:[13]

- Medium to slender physique, and the body frame may be delicate. The Pitta animal shows a medium prominence of veins and muscle tendons. The bones are not as prominent as in the Vata pet.
- Fur is soft and warm, claws are softer.
- They display a medium prominence of eyes.
- Sleep is of medium duration but uninterrupted.
- Paws are warm, bothered by hot weather – it makes them tired, and skin feels warm.
- They pass a large amount of urine.
- Strong metabolism, good digestion with resulting strong appetite and thirst are typical.
- May display irritability if they have to wait for their food or are stressed.
- They have sharp minds and good powers of concentration.
- They are assertive, self-confident, aggressive, demanding, even pushy when out of balance.

---

[13] Ayurveda in Veterinary Medicine | IVC Journal

- Competitive and enjoy challenges, so Pittas make good pack leaders.

Some examples of animals that are predominantly Pitta are muscular cats (lions, panthers, and tigers), eagles, hawks, and snakes. These animals are often fierce, confident, and intelligent, but can also be prone to anger, jealousy, and inflammation.

To balance their Pitta Dosha, they need to avoid excessive heat, spicy foods, and stressful situations, and favor cooling, calming, and sweet foods, and activities.

Pitta is the fire that burns within
The energy that drives metabolism.
The liquid that flows with passion and power;
the Dosha that governs digestion and valor.

Pitta animals are fierce and bold.
They have strong appetites and resist the cold.
They are intelligent and courageous, but can also be
aggressive, and may not do what they're told.

They rule the land and the sky.
They are anything but shy!
Pitta animals need love and respect.
They can teach us to be confident without neglect.

By Carol Ray and Bing A.I

Kapha Dosha in Animals

Kapha is the combination of water and earth. It provides both structure and lubrication. One can visualize Kapha as the stirring force that keeps the water and earth from separating.

Kapha animals are physically strong with a sturdy, heavier build.

- They are aversive to cold, damp weather and may have asthma and allergies
- Have the most energy of all constitutions, but this energy is steady and enduring, not explosive
- Are slow-moving and graceful
- Have soft fur and a tendency for large 'soft' eyes and a soft temperament
- Often overweight though they may eat little; may also suffer from sluggish digestion
- Soft stools, pale in color, and slow evacuation are typical
- Kaphas sleep sound and long.
- They have excellent health, good stamina, and resistance to disease
- Are easy-going, relaxed, slow-paced, happy
- May be slower to learn, but they never forget so they can be possessive, and have a good long-term memory

- **Kapha animals are affectionate and loving, forgiving, compassionate, non-judgmental, stable, reliable, faithful, and are peacemakers**

   Kapha Dosha is the force of cohesion
   that binds the earth and water in union.
   It gives the body strength and stability
   and the mind calmness and tranquility.

   Kapha animals are gentle and loyal.
   They love comfort and avoid turmoil.
   They have a slow but steady pace
   and a sweet tooth and a soft face.

   Kapha animals need balance and care
   to avoid excess weight and despair.
   They should eat light and healthy food
   and exercise to improve their mood.

   Kapha animals are a joy to behold.
   They are compassionate and faithful.
   They are the peacemakers of the world.
   But never pass up a plate for a face-full.

   By Carol Ray & Bing A.I.

Vata Dog   **Pitta Dog**   **Kapha Dog**

Understanding Bodily Functions in Cats and Dogs

According to Dr. Clint G. Rogers in *Ancient Secrets of a Master Healer*, Dr. Pankaj Naram believed that every illness starts with weak digestion and metabolism (low Agni). This creates Aam (toxins) and excess Dosha (imbalance). Excess Dosha and Aam block channels and bodily functions. Finally, tissues become undernourished, and illness is created. The key is to create transformation using the six tools of Siddha-Veda – i.e., diet, home remedies, lifestyle changes, Panchakarma (detoxification), herbal formulas, and Marmaa Shakti to shift imbalances at the root. This holistic approach amazingly supports the entire body system to bring back long-lasting health naturally.

Similar concepts apply to our pets. Eating healthy foods and getting exercise are key to their living their best possible life. The most precious gift you can give your pet or anyone else is your undivided attention. Be present.

"Ancient healing secrets work on human beings, animals, and also plants."

Dr. Pankaj Naram
From Ancient Secrets of a Master Healer (p. 189)

Herbs for Cats & Dogs

Turmeric

Turmeric for animals or people is beneficial for arthritis, diabetes, cancer, liver disease, gastrointestinal issues and more. The curcumin in turmeric is hard for your dog to absorb because it's not soluble in water, so you should combine it with an oil such as coconut oil.

Here are the ingredients and directions you'll need:

You can add the Golden Paste directly to your dog's meals by mixing it with some water or kefir.[14] Most dogs don't mind the taste at all!

- ½ cup organic turmeric powder (make sure it's organic so it contains lots of curcumin and is free of pesticides)
- 1 cup filtered water
- ¼ cup organic, cold-pressed coconut oil
- Optional: add 1 ½ tsp. freshly ground pepper to increase its absorption[15]

Mix the ingredients together in a saucepan and set it on medium/low heat for 5-10 minutes, until it forms a paste. Let the mixture cool, then place it in a jar and store it in the fridge for no more than two weeks.

---

[14] Healing with Turmeric Golden Paste for Dogs

[15] Cancer In Dogs: How To Fight Back With These 3 Herbs

- Small dogs should start with about ¼ tsp./day
- Medium dogs can start with ½ tsp. per day
- Large dogs can start with ¾ tsp. per day
- Giant dogs can start with 1 teaspoon per day

This is a rough starting point, but you can increase the amount from there, up to about a tablespoon for larger dogs.[16] However, you'll want to give turmeric in smaller amounts a few times a day because curcumin leaves the body quickly.

Tulsi

The ancient Vedic texts recommend Tulsi oil to support a healthy inflammatory response in the skin. Manufacturers of veterinary Tulsi supplements recommend roughly 700 mg per dose for dogs, and half that for cats. If an animal is prone to low blood pressure, Tulsi may not be recommended as the herb's calming characteristics may contribute to lowering blood pressure. Tulsi may also slow blood clotting.

Ashwagandha and Neem

Ashwagandha has anti-inflammatory, diuretic, anti-bacterial and anti-fungal properties, plus it is an excellent treatment for anemia. Neem has wonder-

---

[16] Turmeric For Dogs: 5 Surprising Health Benefits - Dogs Naturally (dogsnaturallymagazine.com)

ful anti-inflammatory properties that repel ticks and fleas in a natural and safe manner. Neem is also highly effective for skin problems as it is anti-allergenic and anti-itching.

Benefits of Ashwagandha:

Calming properties: Ashwagandha is classified as an adaptogen, meaning it is non-toxic and a health-promoting plant for a variety of ailments. It reduces stress and helps your dog cope with their fear or anxiety. It enhances the immune system: This plant's immunity-boosting properties are well known and work extremely well for dogs to build their immunity.

- Helps skin and coat: Ashwagandha helps fight skin infections, allergies, hotspots, and itchy skin naturally.[17]

- Relieves pain: It can help relieve pain in your pet's bones, muscles, and joints as it has anti-inflammatory properties.

- Maintains overall health: Ashwagandha maintains the normal function of the nervous and cardiovascular systems, keeping your dog's overall health in check.

- Helps their cognition: It has been found that ashwagandha can enhance cognitive function and improve memory and coordination.

---

[17] Pet care: Why ashwagandha and neem are beneficial for dogs | Lifestyle News - The Indian Express

- Fights tumors: It can help prevent and fight serious diseases like cancer and tumors, too.

General dosage recommendations range from 200 – 500 mg twice daily for cats, and 500 – 1000 mg twice daily for dogs. Note this dosage information is for educational purposes only, and not meant to replace your veterinarian's advice.

Triphala

Adding triphala to your pet's meal can help optimize digestion and absorption of the nutrients being provided. Its properties can also help the respiratory and circulatory systems to function properly. Triphala powder can be given to your pet regularly or as needed.[18]

Cannabis

Both THC (Delta-9-tetrahydrocannbinol) and CBD (Cannabidiol) have been shown in multiple studies to cause apoptosis, or cancer cell suicide, and halt the growth of tumors, in people and animals.[19]

NOTE: Cannabis is still illegal in many places.

---

[18] 5 Ayurvedic Herbs You Can Use to Support Your Pet's Health and Well-Being | Banyan Botanicals

[19] https://www.ncbi.nlm.nih.gov/pmc/articles/PMC3005548

"It's not about how much you do, but how much love you put into what you do that counts."

Saint Mother Teresa of Calcutta
From *Ancient Secrets of a Master Healer*, p. 221

Remedies for Pets

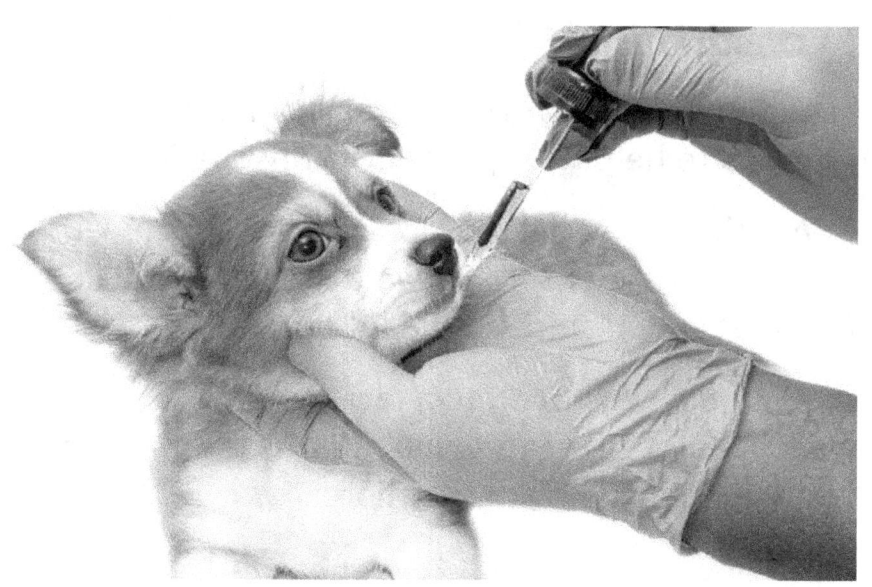

Cat Eye Infection

An eye infection can usually be effectively treated with:

- One 0-capsule of turmeric twice daily as an antibiotic.

Note: a 0-capsule is between 1/16 and 1/8 tsp., an ideal dose for a cat.

Constipation

Adding a spoon of ghee is sometimes all that is required to help with your pet's constipation.

Another potential solution, depending on your dog or cat's appetite, is organic canned pumpkin (without added spices or additives).

Some pets will tolerate a few bits of dried prunes (seeds removed) to their kibble, which should add fiber and help with constipation.

Diarrhea

Withhold solid food until the diarrhea stops or at least slows down. Gradually feed your dog or cat moong bean soup (no onion or garlic) that has been blended to a smooth consistency in small quantities, several times a day. Gradually add back in solid foods.

Some dogs respond well to plain yogurt, without any artificial sugars or Xylitol, which are highly toxic. Try a small spoonful, depending on the size. Seek a vet's assistance for bloody diarrhea or if it persists for more than a few days.

Ear Issues

The health of your dog or cat's ears plays a big part in their auditory experience and overall comfort level. The ear should look pink inside and have a light wax build-up. For general ear maintenance, a drop of a high-quality neem oil on a cotton ball or on your fingertip can be gently applied to the inside of your dog or cat's ear.

If your dog's ears have a distinctly foul odor, it could be a yeast infection in the ear. This is often caused by water or debris trapped in the ear canal, as well as common allergens such as dust, mold, cigarette smoke, pollen, feathers, and household cleaning products. To clean and kill yeast in the ear, use half white vinegar and half filtered water once or twice a day into the ear, using a baby syringe or dropper to apply the solution, or apply to a cotton ball and rub gently around the exterior of the ear if your dog has sensitive ears.

To combat yeast infection of the skin, you can try using Ceylon cinnamon, not Chinese cinnamon, which contains curcumin, a natural blood thinner that can inhibit blood clotting. Mix ⅛ of a teaspoon per 10 pounds of body weight of Ceylon cinnamon with your dog's dry food up to twice a day to banish unwanted skin yeast.

Fleas & Ticks

A few drops of rose geranium oil or neem oil applied to the dog collar can help to repel unwanted ticks and fleas. You could also apply one drop directly behind each shoulder blade and one drop near the base of the tail. Use in a spray with 1 drop geranium oil to 50 drops of carrier oil. The oil mix should be applied every 3 to 5 days. You may have to use more for larger dogs or more stubborn fleas or ticks. It could take 3 to 4 drops to deter these persistent pests. Moderation in all things!

Rose geranium oil is known to lessen fatigue and boost mood, so you get twice the benefits by using this popular essential oil. You should treat your home, pet bedding, carpets, and your vehicle as well if you transport your pets.

Insect Bites

Treat a bee sting or wasp sting by first removing the stinger. One method is to run the edge of a credit card against the bite area to uproot the stinger. Next, make a poultice from one teaspoon of baking soda, cold water, and vinegar.

Apply to the affected area and allow it to sit on the skin for 10 minutes, then rinse it off. Depending on the weather and your dog's temperament, you could also try to create a warm compress using hot water, wring it out, and apply this on top of the baking soda poultice.

For an allergic reaction, give human grade Benadryl™ (one milligram per pound of your dog's weight) every six hours. Benadryl is safe for pets and effective for most allergic reactions in animals and humans.

As with people, it could make your dog drowsy. For swelling, hives or any other severe allergic reaction caused by insect stings, give Benadryl (a pill pocket, piece of cheese, or in a wiener works) and seek immediate emergency care.

Another option for an insect bite with no stinger is a solution made from lavender essential oil and sesame. Lavender oil is an antibiotic, anti-fungal, and anti-bacterial. And as a bonus, it tastes terrible and will prevent licking of the wound in most cases.

Separation Anxiety

Many situations can result in separation anxiety for your pets, particularly after several years of cocooning at home for work and school during these past few years (pandemic).

Physical touch and mental reassurance go a long way, as do going for a long walk or a run before you leave, giving a treat puzzle, calming treats, or having a special weighted blanket, or maybe a shirt that smells like you. One idea is to fake leaving several times daily to get your pet used to you putting on your shoes, picking up your keys, etc.

Vomiting, Belching, and Burping

Try a small piece of ginger root with some honey or ghee for minor stomach issues. Always seek a vet with any signs of persistent vomiting, diarrhea, or bloody diarrhea.

Triphala powder is a good digestive support (in addition to helping with respiratory and circulatory systems). It helps when used as a soothing tonic for a sensitive belly for dogs or cats (and especially people!). The recommended serving size is ¼ teaspoon for every 20 pounds. Start slowly.

To induce vomiting when you know your pet has gotten into something toxic, immediately give your dog a hydrogen peroxide solution of 1 teaspoon per 5 pounds of body weight. This will induce vomiting.

Pets Seizures - Fits & Shakes

Natural remedies are designed to help lessen frequency or severity of seizures, not necessarily alleviate them, although it might be possible if the cause is toxicity (chocolate, caffeine, fruit cores with seeds, ethanol, rat poison, insecticides, and xylitol for examples), heat related, dehydration, or some food allergy. The underlying cause of seizures should always be investigated by a veterinarian before trying natural remedies.

IF YOU SUSPECT POISONING, CALL THE ANIMAL POISON CONTROL CENTER AT (888) 426-4435.

Things to note include what the dog (or cat) was doing before the seizure started, how long it lasted, and the severity of the seizure. Did it affect both sides or only one? Note the recurrence on a calendar so you can provide the vet with as much information as possible. Seizures lasting over 3 minutes or in clusters (recurring or more than 2 within 24 hours) require emergency medical treatments. Some cases of seizures may require prescribed medication by a veterinarian.

Seizures & Coconut Oil

Most dogs can eat coconut oil and anecdotal reports suggest several healthful benefits. But studies suggest that the most impressive gift to dogs is reducing seizures in dogs with epilepsy.[20]

---

[20] Is Coconut Oil Good for Dogs? - Whole Dog Journal (whole-dog-journal.com)

Begin with small amounts and see if anything changes. The recommended amount for most dogs is 1 teaspoon coconut oil per 10 pounds of body weight (1 tablespoon per 30 pounds body weight) daily.

Western Herbs for Seizures

In both capsule and tincture form, many natural over-the-counter herbs including milk thistle, valerian, and oat straw are used to treat seizures. Milk thistle is often recommended by holistic veterinarians to be used in conjunction with phenobarbital. Because it contains antioxidants and has anti-inflammatory properties, this herb helps to treat liver problems which are a side effect of the medication.[21] Valerian root, a mild sedative, and oat straw, a calming herb, can aid dogs suffering from seizures triggered by stress and anxiety.[22]

Be with your dog until he/she gets through the seizure. The longer the seizure, the higher the dog's temperature can go, raising the risk of brain damage. You can help cool the dog's body down by placing an ice pack on the nape of the neck and/or the belly. If you don't have an ice pack you can use ice water on their ears and face. Placing an ice pack on the nape of your dog's neck during a seizure has been shown to lessen the severity and duration of the seizure.

---

[21] [22] 5 Holistic Treatments for Epilepsy in Dogs · The Wildest

After dogs come out of a seizure, their blood sugars can be low. Giving your dog a little all-natural vanilla ice cream, honey, or natural maple syrup will help to raise their sugar levels back up. Follow with a protein such as little kibble, cheese stick, a spoonful of cottage cheese, chicken, etc., to help stabilize those sugar levels.[23]

For additional information:

Natural Seizure Remedies in Dogs - Conditions Treated, Procedure, Efficacy, Recovery, Cost, Considerations, Prevention

https://wagwalking.com/treatment/natural-seizure-remedies

---

[23] Canine Epilepsy: 12 Important Tips if Your Dog Has a Seizure | 4Knines®

Note from Lisa Lowe, Pet Rescue Owner, on Tests & Vets

If you think something's wrong but you are not sure, consider at least getting some blood work done. Consider getting chest X-rays and body X-rays so you will know for sure that everything is good, because dogs are so stoic, they can hide pain for months!

Dr. Naram prescribed detoxing for dogs; you can fast your dog on fruits for a couple of days. Melons and pomegranates are good choices.

You could fast them on water for a day or two, because sometimes just fasting is the cure. Fasting a few days is good medicine.

For most pet parents, it is definitely worth a visit to the vet and lab so you can determine your best course of action.

Lisa Lowe is an animal rescuer from 2009 under Good Deeds-Light Heart Animal Rescue. Specialist in animal nutrition as a master herbalist and alchemist. During her many years of self-study and experience, she continuously pushes the boundaries between traditional veterinary medicine, alternative medicines, and Siddha-Veda (under the guidance of Dr. Pankaj Naram and Dr. Clint G. Rogers).

Pets & Skin Conditions

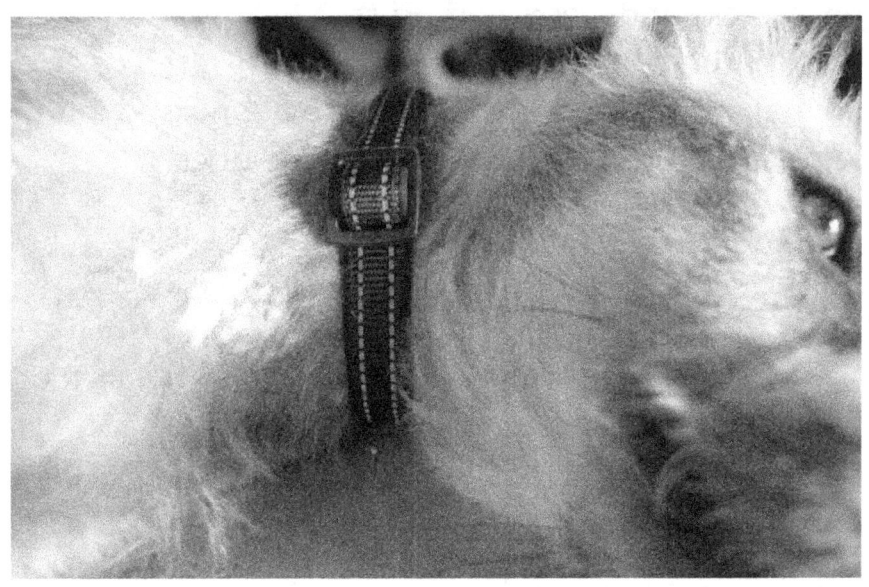

Abscesses

Abscesses are caused by infections when bacteria gets in the skin from a bite, claw, or wound. The infection can spread to the bloodstream if not treated. It might take 3-7 days after a wound for the infection and abscess to set in. If available, this is a good case for a qualified vet to open and drain the abscess and treat if required with antibiotics. In an emergency situation, you can scrub the wound to open it up so the pus will drain out. Be very gentle as too much pressure could cause the infection to enter the bloodstream. Once drained, you can apply heat packs and warm compresses to the wound. This can be a very dangerous situation with an animal in pain, and not wanting to be messed with! A muzzle may be necessary for some dogs.

Mast Cell Tumors

Cancerous tumors on either the top of the skin or beneath the surface.

See Dr. Naram's video on healing a dog with Cushing's Syndrome and a brain tumor: https://youtu.be/4aDUZo45qls

Sebaceous Cyst

A sebaceous cyst is a smaller bump that look like a little pimple or wart that contain an oily substance. If your pet is chewing on the cyst, consider having your pet fitted with a cone. Unless it gets infected, it is harmless.

If it is infected, most respond well to turmeric applied externally. Warm compress can be used to help drain the cyst naturally. Apply 3-4 times daily for 10-15 minutes daily to reduce swelling. Another option is to put castor oil on the cyst, which is an antibacterial, antiviral, and antifungal.

Skin is Too Dry

To soothe a persistent skin itch, try using a chamomile tea spritz daily. Prepare the tea as usual (adjust the amount of water added to the tea bag to lessen or increase potency) and allow it to cool before transferring to a BPA-free spray bottle and refrigerating (3-5 days). Oatmeal paste (made with a little water and finely ground oatmeal) applied to skin for 10 minutes, then rinsed off with warm water, can help to alleviate itch, but your dog may not allow you to get that close to the irritated area. Also consider that the itching may be related to fleas or allergies. Applying a dab of vitamin E oil, neem oil, or lavender oil, can help soothe dry skin.

Pets with Lipomas

— Home Remedy

- ½ Teaspoon Coriander powder
- ½ Teaspoon Cumin powder
- ½ Teaspoon Turmeric powder
- ½ Teaspoon Rock salt powder
- ½ Teaspoon Fenugreek powder
- ¼ Teaspoon Dry Ginger powder
- ¼ Teaspoon Ajwain powder
- 4 pinches of Asafetida powder

Boil all the above-mentioned ingredients in 300 ml (1 ¼ cups) water for 3-4 minutes and then serve it lukewarm. This can be taken/drunk any time, before or after food.

Also: ½ tsp. ghee; ¼ tsp. turmeric; ¼ tsp. black pepper; this works great for furuncles for pups and humans! We (my pup & I) take this morning and night. It makes your skin so soft and clears bumpy yuckies. lol

- Heidi Aden

Dietary Recommendations

Medicine for one can be poison
for another: always start with
VERY SMALL CHANGES
when it comes to your pets.

If thy pet food is:

PROCESSED

CANNED

FROZEN

DEAD

It maketh YOUR PET feel:

FROZEN

CANNED

PROCESSED

DEAD

~ Dr. Pankaj Naram (modified)

Diet for Your Dog

Lean cuts of meat and vegetables are the best choice of food for your dog (if your dog will eat them). Look for cruciferous ones. Broccoli has almost as much protein as steak. Certain vegetables, including cauliflower and turnips, have disease-fighting properties.

Another point to consider is that dogs react to smell. If your dog begins to lose its appetite, lightly season the food with dog-safe spices like cumin, coriander, turmeric, and ginger, just as you would your own food. Never feed your dog onions or garlic unless you have tested the effect on your animal and know exactly how to safely add these.

- Avoid grains or choose food that has as few grains as possible.
- Rice is a good alternative to grains

Other options:

Eliminate as many chemicals from your pet's environment as possible, like pesticides, cleaning products, weed killers, etc.

Do energy work on your pets, like Reiki. You can learn Reiki for yourself and your pets.

Give your pets 100% of your attention when you can. Put down the cell phone, turn off the TV, and make eye contact. Be with your fur baby. Pets love routines and your attention.

Safe & Natural Pet Food

- Natural, sugar-free peanut butter: What dog doesn't love peanut butter? This entertaining snack is fun and will get your dog's tail wagging! Although it's safe for dogs, be careful of portions. Peanut butter has a high-fat content and could lead to weight gain.

- Salmon: Both dogs and cats only get a fraction of the omega-3 that they need. Fresh salmon provides healthy fat, protein, and omegas that they need and is a delicious treat for both cats and dogs!

- Eggs: Eggs are a great source of protein and iron for both dogs and cats! Go ahead and scramble one up when you're making breakfast but be mindful not to add any extra seasoning.

- Watermelon: The benefits of watermelon for dogs? The fruit itself is a health-food powerhouse, low in calories and packed with nutrients—vitamins A, B6, and C, and potassium. Plus, fruit has only about 50 calories a cup and 92 percent water, so it's great for hydration on a hot day. It also has no fat or cholesterol, so it's pretty much guilt-free.[24]

- Apples: Apples are another great treat, but make sure to remove the seeds and the core from this vitamin A and vitamin C packed treat.

---

[24] 10 Best Fruits That Your French Bulldog Needs To Eat

Apples are great because they help to clean residue off your dog's teeth and will help to freshen his breath! If your dog doesn't like apples, try a small piece with a bit of peanut butter.

- Broccoli: This may be a tough sell, but some dogs do enjoy broccoli! Broccoli is high in fiber and vitamin C and is low in fat so it makes it a safe and nutritious treat for your dog. You can serve it raw or cooked if no seasoning is added! Puppies may not be capable of digesting raw broccoli.
- Carrots: These veggies are a perfect, low calorie, and crunchy snack! Carrots are chock-full of vitamins, minerals, and fiber. Just be mindful of giving your dog manageable pieces that they can safely eat without choking.
- Peas: Green peas are a great healthy treat and are commonly found as an ingredient in many dog food brands.
- Avocados: Avocado provides vitamins A, C, E, and B6 which is great for your cat's skin and coat. The risk in feeding pets avocado is due to the high fat content that can affect the pancreas. It can also cause upset tummies and diarrhea. Portions should be kept small for your cats as avocados are higher in fat. And, of course, make sure the skin and pit are entirely removed before serving it to your pets as they contain persin, which is unsafe for pets.

- Pumpkin: Pumpkin is a great superfood, and a perfect treat during the fall and winter! It's packed full of nutrients and even helps keep their skin and coat strong and healthy.
- Pumpkin Seeds: When giving pumpkin seeds to your dogs, it is best to serve them cleaned, peeled, roasted, and ground. Do not let your pets eat raw seeds!
- Ghee: Offer a teaspoon of Ghee to your HEALTHY pets in the morning before their breakfast. They love licking it off the spoon! Ghee helps build strong bones and lubricates the hips and joints. Ghee is also full of vitamin A. And that's great for your dog's immune system. Ghee can help improve brain health and cognitive functions such as vision. However, pets with diabetes, or other disorders may have difficulty in digesting ghee.
- Cheese: Who doesn't love a little cheddar or mozzarella? But keep in mind, consumption should be very limited (much to the dismay of canines everywhere!). Many dogs have lactose intolerance, and if they overdo it, it may cause a tummy upset.
- Yogurt or Kefir: Another dairy treat, unflavored and unsweetened yogurt or kefir is a great healthy treat that will give your dog some healthy probiotics. And what dog doesn't love licking a spoon? Try freezing yogurt/kefir with

some fruit to give him a nice refreshing treat! Since yogurt/kefir are dairy treats, remember to limit them for dogs with lactose intolerance!

Cats and Vegetables

- Try to feed your cat some cut-up vegetables! Cats need fiber. If they won't have it, grow or buy some cat-friendly plants and make them accessible.
- You might also explore feeding your cat some baked or steamed carrots, squash, or broccoli to get that fiber fix. For cats, no seasonings.

Special Diet for Sick and/or Elderly Cats (Baby Food)

- For elderly, sickly, or cats with dental issues: Stage 1 Meats include chicken in broth, turkey in broth, and beef in broth. These recipes contain just meat and broth, so they should be safe for your cat.
- Most are free from starch and should meet your cat's natural carnivorous needs.

2nd Stage Baby Foods: Meats and Gravy

This product lineup includes ham, turkey, chicken, and beef recipes. They're all made without any garlic, onions, or other seasonings. The simple recipes include just meat, water, and cornstarch.

While cornstarch isn't ideal for cats, it can be an acceptable inclusion in their diet if the cat is sick or otherwise in desperate need of nutrition.

Baby Food You SHOULD NOT Feed Your Cat

Before you feed your cat baby food, read the ingredient list. Don't give your kitty any food containing the following ingredients:

- Onion
- Garlic
- Added sugars or sweeteners
- Canola oil or other vegetable oils
- Certain vegetables like, tomatoes, onions, garlic, chives
- Salt
- Dairy (goat's milk is okay)

Check with other commercially available baby food companies, checking for additives and preservatives.

How long can you feed your cat baby food?

- Your cat can eat baby food alone for about 2-3 days before you'll need to start transitioning your kitty back to a nutritionally complete and balanced raw, homemade, gently cooked, or canned diet.

For additional information: Can Cats Eat Baby Food? Best Baby Food for Cats - Wildernesscat

Moong for Mutts & Mews - Carol Ray

- 30% Cooked and sprouted moong beans
- 5% Salmon oil
- 4% Scrambled egg
- 10% Carrots, peas, green beans, dandelion greens
- ½% Ghee
- ¼% Ashwagandha, liquid
- ¼% Turmeric powder
- 50% Rice as a carb

This is just an idea for a situation where packaged, store-bought food isn't available. It is a starting point. This can be mixed using an electric mixer or by hand. Portions can be wrapped individually and refrigerated for convenience. Add or subtract for your fur baby's preferences or health needs.

Unsafe Foods for Pets

- Chocolate: You are likely aware of this common unsafe food for your pet, but it must be mentioned! Chocolate is toxic to both dogs and cats because of the chemical theobromine and could lead to death. Not only should you not serve chocolate to your pet, but you should also keep it stored in a place far from their reach.

- Grapes: Most people don't know this, but besides being a choking hazard, grapes are highly toxic to your pets. Consumption of even a small amount of grapes could lead to kidney failure and death.

- Nuts: Macadamia nuts are intolerable and can make your pet miserable. While they are unlikely to lead to death, they will undoubtedly lead to significant health issues and make for an unhappy pup. Also avoid almonds, pecans, and pistachios.

- Seeds: avoid feeding your dog sunflower seeds and raw pumpkin seeds.

- Garlic, onions, chives, and leeks are all in the Allium genus of plants AND SHOULD NOT BE FED TO DOGS. Garlic, whether raw or cooked, is considered by most vets to be toxic to dogs. However, some people have had success feeding tiny amounts of fresh, minced garlic to their dogs without incident.

- If a cat eats enough garlic, it can eventually kill them if they do not get medical treatment. Onions are harmful to dogs. If your dog gets into an onion, they may experience anemia, gastroenteritis, and/or damage to red blood cells. (Dogs are not allergic to plants in this genus, but the plants contain N-propyl disulfides and thiosulfates).[25]

- Mushrooms: MOST STORE-BOUGHT MUSHROOMS ARE SAFE FOR DOGS. But wild mushrooms can be highly dangerous and toxic. The most common form of documented mushroom poisoning in dogs is toxicity resulting from the Death Cap in the Amanita species. It is believed that canines are attracted to members of this species because of their fishy odor. It may be hard to confirm if your pet has ingested wild mushrooms unless you see your dog eat them, or he vomits mushrooms. At the earliest suspicion of ingestion, immediately go to the veterinarian clinic or emergency room. If possible, bring a sample of the mushroom in a paper (not plastic) bag as mushroom identification is helpful to diagnosis. In particular, the amanita phalloides (otherwise known as death cap) are most toxic.

- Ingestion of mushrooms can be highly toxic and a potentially life-threatening occurrence for your pet. The accumulation of toxins in your dog's system can lead to kidney and liver failure, and quite possibly coma and death. If you

---

[25] Can Dogs Eat Garlic? | PetMD

suspect your dog has eaten wild mushrooms, do not wait for symptoms to appear. Take your pet to the veterinarian immediately for early identification of the mushroom type. Identification, and prompt emergency measures to reduce the toxicity levels in your dog's system are crucial steps towards recovery.[26]

- Cooked Bones: A lot of dog owners will hand over a bone once it's been picked clean. However, you should know that cooked bones can easily splinter. When a bone splinters, it can cause these splinters to enter the dog's intestinal track and cause some nasty damage. Instead, it is better to give raw bones! It is also recommended to talk with your vet about some chew toys or products that are safer for your pet, especially depending on his age, teeth condition, or chewing tendencies

- Raw eggs are not recommended for dogs (although others may believe they are harmless) and are considered unsafe for several reasons. First, raw eggs may be contaminated with bacteria and can transmit infections including E. coli and Salmonella. It has been shown that the risk of Salmonella is significantly greater in dogs fed raw eggs. Not only can these bacteria cause serious illness in dogs (and their owners), but these infections may be hard to treat.[27]

---

[26] Mushroom Poisoning in Dogs - Symptoms, Diagnosis, Treatment

[27] Can Dogs Eat Eggs? | Great Pet Care

- In addition to the food safety concerns, there are nutritional concerns with respect to raw eggs. Egg white contains a protein called avidin, which binds biotin, a B-vitamin. Biotin is not considered an essential nutrient for dogs, meaning it doesn't need to be present in their diet as dogs can synthesize it themselves. Yet, feeding raw eggs can induce biotin deficiency as the synthesized biotin is bound by the avidin and cannot be utilized by the dog.

- Eggshells: It is not recommended to feed eggshells to dogs. Eggshells are composed predominantly of calcium carbonate, which is a very calcium-rich, highly digestible compound. This provides a large dose of calcium in addition to the calcium provided in a dog's main diet. Calcium recommendations are quite strict for dogs and even more so for growing puppies. Adding extra dietary calcium can easily imbalance the diet, especially from a source such as eggshell that is rich in calcium but deficient in phosphorus. The imbalance of the calcium to phosphorus ratio can impact vitamin D status and have effects on skeletal metabolism.[28]

- An alternative for calcium is to feed ground sesame seeds. Try a small amount, up to a half teaspoon a day, sprinkled on their kibble. Always look for signs of allergi reaction to something new, or for abdominal discomfort.

---

[28] How much bone meal should I give my dog? (thefaithfuldog.com)

- Alcohol: Alcohol has the same effect on dogs as in people but in much smaller doses. For those of you with cats, it's even more imperative that you don't try to party with your feline friend. Even trace amounts of alcohol can lead to severe brain damage or liver failure.

- Aspartame and Xylitol: You won't find these chemicals in your fridge, but you will find them in some processed foods. If you're feeding your dog anything that has a label, be sure to look for these chemicals. They are sugar substitutes, and most are found in baked goods, yogurt, gum, and candy. Even small amounts of consumption could lead to dangerous drops in blood pressure, kidney failure, and death.

Just as anything can be a poison or a medicine, your pet's diet should be specific to your pet's health, likes, activity levels, and to availability in your area. Check with your vet before making any major changes to your pet's diet.[29]

Dog Food Advisor – provides updates on food that has been recalled: (https://www.dogfoodadvisor.com/recall-alert-confirmation/) and can give you a run down on the ingredients in the food you are buying: https://www.dogfoodadvisor.com/dog-food/reviews/

---

[29] Can Dogs Eat Raw Meat? | PetMD

Making Your Own Dog Food - Lisa Lowe

Lisa Lowe is an animal rescuer since 2009 under Good Deeds-Light Heart Animal Rescue. Specialist in animal nutrition as a master herbalist and alchemist. During her many years of self-study and experience, she continuously pushes the boundaries between traditional veterinary medicine, alternative medicines, and Siddha-Veda (under the guidance of Dr. Pankaj Naram and Dr. Clint G. Rogers).

Homemade Dog Kibble

What you need to make your own Moong Kibble/Dry Food:

Equipment/Tools:

- Dehydrator (alternative: oven method)
- Cookie sheet
- Parchment paper or 1 tsp. ghee for pan
- Grinder
- Blender
- Pastry tube (cake frosting tube)

Ingredients:

- ½ cup green moong beans
- Dash of black salt
- 1 cup cubes sweet potato (peeled)
- ½ cup blueberries
- 1 cup dandelion greens (washed, stems removed)

- 1 cup fresh carrots - grated or chopped finely
- 1 tsp. ghee
- ¼ tsp. cumin
- ¼ tsp. grated ginger
- ¼ tsp. turmeric
- 2 ounces beef or chicken broth or bone broth*

***Note about Broth & Pets**

Even "low sodium"-branded broths may be too high in sodium levels for many dogs, so using commercial broth is not recommended in pets with medical conditions. Also be sure to check for other ingredients in commercial broths that may be yummy to us but are toxic to pets (onions, garlic, sugar, etc.).

Option to make your own broth:

The safest recipe is boiling unseasoned meat [and] or vegetables in plain water to form a basic broth. However, because there is no way to determine the nutrient profile of your homemade broth, owners should always consult their veterinarian to make sure the ingredients you use are not harmful for your pet.

Take-Away: Adding broth to your pet's food can be a tasty, low calorie addition to your pet's diet. But as with any diet change, it is always important to consult your veterinarian first!

Written in conjunction with veterinary student, Rachel Hanford.

https://vetnutrition.tufts.edu/2020/10/boiling-it-down-adding-broth-to-your-pets-meals/

Directions to make Moong Flour:

Soak moong (mung) beans overnight or until they are about to sprout. Rinse thoroughly.

Cook beans on the stove top in 4 cups of water for 45 minutes or longer (until soft) or in a pressure cooker according to manufacturer's instructions, with a dash of black salt.

Don't overcook the beans! Once cooked, rinse, strain, and put in a dehydrator. Leave them in the dehydrator for 4-6 hours depending on the machine.

Dehydrator Alternative: Put the beans on a cookie sheet on a wire rack in the middle of the oven, with the temperature set to its lowest setting, typically 180 degrees Fahrenheit (about 82 degrees Celsius) for 60 minutes, until the beans are dry and firm. Temperature varies with appliance. Take beans out and put them in a blender or coffee grinder.

Congratulations! You just made moong flour!

Making Kibble

To a 2-quart pan, add diced sweet potato, blueberries, dandelion greens, and green beans (strings and ends removed and snapped into 2" pieces).

In a saucepan, add 1 tsp. ghee on low heat then add herbs: cumin, turmeric, and grated ginger and sauté for 3-4 minutes.

Add 1 cup moong floor, cooked vegetables, and herbs in a blender. Use the pulse setting until the mixture is blended. You can add a bit of water if needed or veggie broth or meat broth, as the mixture should be firm enough to hold its shape, but not be runny.

Put about a ⅛th cup of the mixture into a pastry tube (cake frosting tube) and make small dollops of kibble on the dehydrator paper. Repeat until the pan is full.

Place in the dehydrator on a low setting (145-160° F or 57-70° C) for 60 minutes. Let it dehydrate to a semi-firm kibble size. Take out and store it in an airtight container. Time varies by appliance.

Alternate Method: put the kibble mixture from the cake frosting tube on parchment paper lining a baking sheet. Bake on 350 degrees for 15-20 minutes, depending on the kibble size. The kibble is done when it's firm and holds its shape. Store in an air-tight container.

I prefer dehydrators and making small bits depending on the size of the dog(s).

Congratulations! You just made homemade kibble!

You can make biscuits as well and you can change the recipe based on the dog's health issues and appetite.

You can also use different fruits and veggies and dehydrate them and make them into a powder so you can add them when needed to your recipes.

See list of safe fruits and vegetables on page 142.

On the following pages, Lisa Lowe shares some of her specific recipes for cardiovascular and kidney issues.

Recipes for Cardiovascular Issues

Cardiovascular - Low Sodium, Heart-Healthy Recipe Option 1 (Salmon)

- 330 grams (⅔ pound) of Salmon, cooked
- 3 cups rice, quinoa or millet
- 1 large egg, hardboiled
- ½ cup green beans
- 1-3 Spinach leaves, raw
- 1 tsp. cod liver oil, optional
- 3 tsp. Safflower oil
- ⅛ cup optional organic tomato sauce or fresh tomatoes mashed or blended

Cook the salmon and let it cool.

Cook the rice, quinoa, or millet.

Hard boil the egg and mash.

Pulse the green beans and spinach leaves with the cod liver oil and safflower oil.

Add this mixture to the rice/quinoa/millet, and mix in the salmon.

Add tomato sauce or the mashed or blended tomatoes (seeds, stems, and skin rememoved).

Cardio Herbal Blend - Recipe 2 (Chicken & Chicken Liver)

- 245 g (½ pound) raw chicken breast to cook
- 145 g (⅓ pound) chicken liver, cooked
- 1 ½ apples skinned and sliced
- ⅔ cup blueberries
- 1 cup raw broccoli
- 10 Brussel sprouts
- 1 cup cabbage
- 1 tsp. cod liver oil
- 5 Tbsp. of moong beans, blended as butter
- 3 tsp. safflower oil
- 4 tsp. ghee
- ⅛ cup tomato sauce or mashed tomatoes

Poach chicken until tender.

Cook chicken liver until they break apart.

Pulse in a blender with apples, blueberries, broccoli, Brussels sprouts, cabbage, and moong beans, the cod liver oil, safflower oil, and ghee into small bits.

Add tomato sauce or tomatoes (seeds, stems, and skin rememoved) mashed with herbal cardio blend and liver, and mix.

Cardio Herbal Blend - Recipe 3 (Fish)

- 1 ¼ cups moong beans
- 240 g (½ pound) flat fish/sole cooked
- 2 large eggs hard boiled
- ⅓ cup of almonds grounded
- 1 ¼ cup broccoli, raw chopped
- ¾ cups raw carrots
- 1 tsp. cod liver oil
- 5 tsp. safflower oil
- 4 tsp. Ghee
- 1 cup tomatoes, cherry raw

Prepare the moong beans and cook for 45 minutes after sprouting the previous day.

Poach the fish.

Hard boil the eggs and mash.

Pulse the almonds, broccoli, carrots, tomatoes, cod liver oil, safflower oil, and Ghee into small bits.

Add this mixture to the beans and then mix in the fish.

Cardio Herbal Blend - Recipe 4 (Beef)

- 1 ½ cup moong beans cooked.
- 245 g (about ½ pound) beef, ground cooked
- 2 large eggs hard boiled
- ¼ cup blueberries
- 1 ½ cup broccoli, raw chopped
- ½ cup raw carrots
- ½ cup peas thawed
- 2-3 leaves of spinach
- ½ tsp. cod liver oil
- 3 tsp. safflower oil
- 3 tsp. ghee

Prepare the moong beans and cook for 45 minutes after sprouting the previous day.

Cook the beef.

Hard boil the eggs and mash.

Pulse the blueberris, broccoli, carrots, peas, spinach, cod liver oil, safflower oil, and Ghee into small bits.

Add this mixture to the beans and then mix in the beef.

Cardio Herbal Blend - Recipe 5 (Chicken)

- 1 ¼ cup rice, quinoa or millet
- 225 g (about ½ pound) chicken breast
- 4 large hard-boiled eggs
- 1 ½ cup broccoli
- 6 Brussel sprouts
- 1 cup peas
- ½ tsp. cod liver oil
- 3 tsp. safflower oil
- 3 tsp. ghee

Cook the rice, quinoa, or millet.

Cook the chicken breast.

Hard boil the eggs and mash.

Pulse the broccoli, Brussel sprouts, peas, cod liver oil, safflower oil, and Ghee into small bits.

Add this mixture to the rice/quinoa/millet, and mix in the chicken breast.

*All recipes can have the vegetables steamed for easier digestion while your dog is transitioning the diet.

Dogs with Kidney issues

Kidneys are a vast subject. The diet depends on whether the issue is low, weak energy, kidney stones, backend weakness in hind legs. The following basic recipes are for low kidney function with low Phosphorus.

- 1 ½ cup of egg white or moong beans
- 1 ⅓ cup of green beans
- ½ cup of pears, cubed
- 7 leaves spinach or dandelion leaves
- 5 Tbsp. of ghee
- 2 tsp. cod liver oil
- 4 Tbsp. manuka honey
- 3 ½ Tbsp. safflower oil
- 1 Tbsp. seaweed or kelp
- ¼ cup of firm tofu with calcium sulfate

Prepare and blend like in the previous recipes by cooking the beans and blending the rest of the ingredients before mixing them togetther.

Supplement with 150 mg potassium citrate a day..

Feeding Guide

lbs. dog	kg	calories/day	grams/day	cups
5	2.3	231	121	¾
10	4.5	389	204	1 ½
15	6.8	527	277	2 ⅛
20	9.1	654	343	2 ⅔
25	11.4	774	406	3 ⅛
30	13.6	887	466	3 ⅔
For larger dogs double the recipes				

Recipe 2

- 1 ⅔ cup egg whites cooked or moong beans
- 1 ⅓ cup green beans boiled
- 7 leaves spinach or dandelion leaves
- ½ cup pears
- 5 Tbsp. ghee
- 2 tsp. cod liver
- 1 tsp. safflower
- ⅓ cup of firm tofu with calcium sulfate

Prepare as described above and supplement with potassium citrate 150 mg a day.

Recipe 3

- 220 g (about ½ pound) of chicken breast cooked
- 1 ⅛ egg whites or moong beans
- 1 ⅔ cup green beans
- 9 leaves spinach, or dandelion leaves
- ⅜ cup pears
- 5 Tbsp. ghee
- 2 tsp. cod liver oil
- 2 Tbsp. manuka honey
- 8 tsp. safflower oil

Prepare as described in the basic Kidney recipe and supplement with potassium citrate 150 mg a day.

Feeding Guide

lbs	kg	calories/day	grams/day	cups
10	4.5	389	288	2 ¼
20	9.1	654	384	2 ¾
30	13.6	887	520	3 ¾
40	18.2	1101	645	4 ¾
50	22.7	1301	763	5 ¾

Recipe 4

- 330 g (⅔ pound) chicken breast
- ¾ cups egg whites or moong beans
- 1 ⅓ green beans or zucchini
- 7 leaves spinach or dandelion leaves
- 1 cup pears
- 3 Tbsp. ghee
- 2 tsp. cod liver oil
- 3 Tbsp. manuka honey
- 10 tsp. safflower oil
- ¼ cup yogurt plain organic

Prepare as described in the basic Kidney recipe and supplement with potassium citrate 150 mg a day.

Some of these recipes are just interchanging a meat, egg white or tofu substitute.

"When we think of those companions
who travelled by our side down life's road,
let us not say with sadness
that they left us behind,
but rather say with gentle gratitude
that they once were with us."

~ Unknown

Our Final Gift - Dr. Susan Engman

Some believe that there is no final chapter in the relationship with our beloved. But inevitably they do leave their bodies and it is the end of their life. While this can be emotionally challenging, we offer these important considerations to help you and your loved ones feel more empowered and comforted.

The mutual relationship you have with your animal continues throughout time. Animals have souls that stay connected to you even when they are no longer in physical form. You carry them with you in your heart and memories for the rest of your time.

A relationship with a beloved animal is profound. Our animals provide unconditional love and acceptance, physical touch, a soul connection, a best friend, a source of nurturance and support. They can be our external hearts.

Feelings of loss and grief are normal and universal at a time of loss. Unfortunately, in some cultures people minimize and dismiss the feelings of grief and loss that can come from the death of an animal friend. If you experience people not honoring what you are going through, realize that they have not had the blessing of such a relationship.

Do not look to them to understand and comfort you. Their reaction is about them, not a judgment about you. There are so many people who will deeply understand what you are going through and offer compassion. For additional support and understanding to know that you are not alone, search online. There are plenty of resources available such as support groups, books, videos, movies and people to talk with personally.

Any and all feelings you have around the loss of your beloved animal is normal and important. Embrace your feelings and know that they are valid. The pain is real and will pass with time.

If, after a significant amount of time you are feeling immobilized by your grief do contact a counselor. A few sessions can help you resolve whatever is necessary to feel yourself again. Know that your animal would want you to be happy.

Your best ally in knowing when it is time to say goodbye is your animal. Dying is an organic process meaning that your animal will most likely let you know it is time to go. Their world gets smaller, many will stop eating and drinking. Some show pain behaviors. (It's good to know what those signs look like; ask your veterinarian, or look up how pain presents in your breed's body). They can lose control of bodily functions, bladder, bowel, or the ability to move around.

One of the hardest decisions in this process is knowing when it is time to help your animal leave their bodies. This is our opportunity to return the friendship they have offered us. Often folks witness a slow decline and find themselves unable to see when their beloved animal begins to deeply suffer. This is a time to have support. Ask others to let you know what they are seeing in your animal.

Know that letting them go to avoid intense pain or suffering is an act of love. We have this gift to offer to our dear friend at this moment. No matter when you decide, know that the love you both shared lives on in your heart and in their soul.

In some acute situations, the veterinarian may strongly advise you to take your animal out of agony. This will come as a shock to you but out of the love you have for your animal, it is time to humanely agree. In this kind of difficult situation, you can call someone close to you to provide whatever support you need. Let yourself feel your feelings. Crying is very normal. Heartache is normal. Your veterinarian can give you privacy to have a final goodbye with your animal where you share with gratitude all the love you have together. At the deepest level your animal knows that their transition time is here. They will be comforted to say goodbye with love. If you can, stay with them as they are given the medication. It is normally a peaceful process, not one to be feared. As I write this, I feel the pain in my heart and have tears in my eyes remembering all the animals I have loved and said goodbye to. It is a good heartache which reminds me how much I have loved and been loved by them.

If your veterinarian tells you it is time to let them go and it is not a crisis situation, please give yourself time and permission to say goodbye in your own way. If you and your pet need more time, do not be rushed into it. That may mean taking your pet home and calling the ones who have been close to say goodbye in their own way. This can make such a big difference for your animal's other friends and family members. If it feels appropriate, children can be involved as well. Death is a normal part of life and saying goodbye to loved ones can be a profoundly important learning/growth experience for everyone.

It is very helpful to have done some research before the time comes to know if there are mobile vet services available in your area. If possible, this is the most comfortable option for everyone involved, especially your pet. It is also good to know about burial and cremation choices, including costs. In the moment of passing it is challenging to navigate these kinds of decisions and conversations; doing so ahead of time can be helpful and perhaps can lessen the stress.

Once the difficult decisions have been made, your final act of love and gratitude is to comfort them as they pass from this life. You can touch them, talk to them, even sing. Crying is beautiful as well. Give them permission to go, the peace of knowing you are going to be alright, and that the love you share will live on forever.

A good cry as a family and saying words of love and appreciation matter. Have children do artwork about their feelings, read books about animals dying (many such children's books are available, just look online) and continue to talk about the pet after they die is important in the grieving process. This is true for the grownups as well. Consider lighting a candle together at the time of death for safe passage and comfort for all. Any rituals you come up with from your tradition help support the healing process and matter.

Don't be surprised at the multiple ways your animal shows up for you after they have left their body. They might come in dreams, or you may have a sense that they are in the room, you might see them out of the corner of your eye. These are all reminders that their Spirit and love is still very much alive and with you. What a blessing the journey has been.

My brother, who always had two dogs, said, "the best way to recover from the loss and sadness of losing a dog is to get a puppy!". Not to replace or diminish the significance of grief and loss but in celebration of the love you still have to share and receive. That may be extreme for some and exactly the right answer for others.

Some find themselves experiencing such significant pain and loss that they say they will never again have a pet because it hurts too much when they die. In that moment, the pain of loss overrides the years of loving companionship and the great joy of sharing life with animals.

Each animal, like every human relationship, is unique and provides a unique experience of love. You can never have the same relationship you had with your departed animal, but we invite you to be open and allow a new and beautiful love to possibly be channeled through another animal in your life. Animals bring such joy and richness into our lives, and they provide something so unique and special. The depth of our grief and loss is an indicator of the depth of the love and connection we are able to experience. Listen within you for the quiet voice which lets you know if it is time for a new friend to be brought into your life. This is always mutual. You will absolutely be enriched, and you could literally be saving an animal's life in the process.

Charities We Love That Support Animals

Nepal Orphan Kids – 100% to the kids!
https://www.zeffy.com/en-US/donation-form/0d90e804-ede9-4e03-97b5-2662af26e58a

Homeless Dogs in India:
https://www.AncientSecretsFoundation.org/product/atithi-devo-bhava-donation/

Wildlife SOS
Refuse to Ride Petition for Elephants – Contact https://action.wildlifesos.org/page/74446/action/1?ea.tracking.id=refusetoride

Saving Wild Horses: Wild Horse Fire Brigade:
Contact Peggy Coleman Taylor: FlyNorth@att.net
Wildhorsefirebrigade.org

Keep Wild Horses Wild – Peggy Coleman Taylor

Under public law 92-195, "It is the policy of Congress that wild free-roaming horses and burros shall be protected from capture, branding, harassment, or death..." Wild horses have complex ecological, social, and behavioral needs; there is an understanding of traits that are specific to wild animals. WILD HORSES belong in their natural habitats and not in the hands of private individuals as "pets".

The Bureau of Land Management (BLM) and United States Forest Service (USFS) mismanagement of wild horses and burros, via roundups and sterilization will ultimately result with a lack of genetic DNA diversity and eventually led to a die-off of these American icons of the West. Presently, there are more wild horses in BLM holding facilities than remain in the wild.

The BLM Adoption Incentive Program (AIP) is a failure to thousands of wild horses ending up in the slaughter pipeline. In 2023, the WILDHORSE FIRE BRIGADE, an all-volunteer 501(c)(3) non-profit focused on preserving the wild horse from extinction has re-wilded 70+ American Native horses rescued from slaughter who were supposed to be Federally protected.

The better solution for "excess" wild horses is to re-wild them in wilderness areas that are not in conflict with livestock or mining (also known as LAND GRABS) and be put to "work" as nature's fire mitigators. Horses being large herbivores naturally protect the land's ecosystems.

Wildhorse Fire Brigade's pilot program, using the Jane Goodall method for collecting scientific data of wild horses, is proving to be an important part of the wildfire solution, environmentally and economically.

Science supports the fact that vegetative fuel reduction reduces both the frequency, size, and intensity of catastrophic wildfires.

Per H.R. 4821-417 (formerly H.R. 1625-313) Humane transfer of excess animals SEC 113... whereas, the Secretary of Interior may transfer "excess" wild horses and burros that have been removed from public land to other government agencies for use as work animals.

7,000 Lost Freedom and Family
BLM-Broken Arrow, Fallon, NV

Other countries realize the benefits of using wild horses for fire mitigation.

Little money is allocated to fund the study of American native wild horses. STOP the round ups, sterilization, and adoption of WILD horses! Please support the WILD HORSE FIRE BRIGADE, a better solution.

Wildlife SOS – Refuse to Ride Elephants

It may be your dream to ride an elephant, but it is an elephant's worst nightmare to be ridden.

Here's what goes into making an elephant "rideable." First, an elephant calf is captured from the wild, tearing it away from its mother and herd — as well as from any chance it has of a free, wildlife. This is illegal and can be termed as "poaching."

After the capture, the elephant is kept in isolation for all its life with no or little interaction with other elephants. This is psychologically detrimental for the elephant, causing it to become withdrawn and unhappy.

Once in captivity, these elephants are often neglected and poorly cared for. They receive little or no veterinary care; their nutrition is compromised, and they have restricted access to water.

These captive elephants are chained for extended periods of time, often standing in their own dung and urine.

The very act of riding is cruel — an elephant's back was not designed to carry weight and yet the weight of the carrier, the mahout/keeper, and the tourists on its back, can put an intense amount of pressure on the animal's spine. These weights can often exceed 200-400 kilograms (440-880 pounds)

of the howdah and in addition to it the weight of the mahout and three adult passengers easily exceeds 600 kilograms (about 1,300 pounds) — causing sores, bruises, cuts, and deformities in the animal's back, but most importantly, it leads to early arthritis and severe joint pains.

https://action.wildlifesos.org/page/74446/action/1?ea.tracking.id=refusetoride

References

[1] 5 Ayurvedic Herbs You Can Use to Support Your Pet's Health and Well-Being
https://www.banyanbotanicals.com/info/blog-the-banyan-insight/details/5-herbs-for-pets/

[2] Balance your horse with these ayurvedic herbs
https://equinewellnessmagazine.com/ayurvedic-herbs/

[3] Essential Oil and Liquid Potpourri Poisoning in Cats
https://vcahospitals.com/know-your-pet/essential-oil-and-liquid-potpourri-poisoning-in-cats

[4] Essential Oils for Cats: Benefits, Risks, & Considerations
https://www.veterinarians.org/are-essential-oils-safe-for-cats/

[5] Dr. Pankaj Naram: Healthy Diet Recommendations
https://issuu.com/dr.pankajnaram/docs/drpankaj_f019a4ca75bc42

[6] Veterinary Ayurveda: Case Histories of Five Cats
http://ayurveda.alandiashram.org/ayurvedic-treatment/veterinary-ayurveda-cats

[7] [8] Ayurveda in Veterinary Medicine
https://ivcjournal.com/ayurveda-veterinary-medicine/

[9] [10] [11] Ayurveda in Veterinary Medicine | IVC Journal
https://ivcjournal.com/ayurveda-veterinary-medicine/

[12] Ayurveda For Animals (dogsnaturallymagazine.com)
https://www.dogsnaturallymagazine.com/ayurveda-for-animals/

[13] Ayurveda in Veterinary Medicine | IVC Journal
https://ivcjournal.com/ayurveda-veterinary-medicine/

[14] Healing with Turmeric Golden Paste for Dogs
https://www.dogsnaturallymagazine.com/healing-with-turmeric-golden-paste-for-dogs/

[15] Cancer In Dogs: How To Fight Back With These 3 Herbs
https://bensbarketplace.com/cancer-dogs-fight-back-3-herbs/

[16] Turmeric For Dogs: 5 Surprising Health Benefits - Dogs Naturally (dogsnaturallymagazine.com)
https://www.dogsnaturallymagazine.com/turmeric-dogs/

[17] Pet care: Why ashwagandha and neem are beneficial for dogs | Life-style News - The Indian Express
https://indianexpress.com/article/lifestyle/life-style/pet-care-ashwagandha-neem-beneficial-for-dogs-7669463/

[18] Ayurvedic Herbs You Can Use to Support Your Pet's Health and Well-Being
https://www.banyanbotanicals.com/info/blog-the-banyan-insight/details/5-herbs-for-pets/

[19] Cannabinoid-induced apoptosis in immune cells as a pathway to immunosuppression
https://www.ncbi.nlm.nih.gov/pmc/articles/PMC3005548

[20] Is Coconut Oil Good for Dogs? - Whole Dog Journal
https://www.whole-dog-journal.com/nutrition/is-coconut-oil-good-for-dogs/

[21] [22] 5 Holistic Treatments for Epilepsy in Dogs · The Wildest
https://www.thewildest.com/dog-health/holistic-treatments-epilepsy-dogs

[23] Canine Epilepsy: 12 Important Tips if Your Dog Has a Seizure
https://4knines.com/blogs/4knines-blog-home-page/canine-epilepsy-12-important-tips-dog-seizure

[24] 10 Best Fruits That Your French Bulldog Needs To Eat
https://www.frenchbulldogbreed.net/blog/10-best-fruits-for-your-french-bulldog/

[25] Can Dogs Eat Garlic?
https://www.petmd.com/dog/nutrition/can-dogs-eat-garlic

[26] Mushroom Poisoning in Dogs - Symptoms, Diagnosis, Treatment
https://wagwalking.com/condition/mushroom-poisoning

[27] Can Dogs Eat Eggs? | Great Pet Care
https://www.greatpetcare.com/dog-nutrition/can-dogs-eat-eggs-info-on-raw-cooked-and-egg-shells/

[28] How much bone meal should I give my dog? (thefaithfuldog.com)
https://thefaithfuldog.com/how-much-bone-meal-should-i-give-my-dog/

[29] Can Dogs Eat Raw Meat? | PetMD
https://www.petmd.com/dog/nutrition/can-dogs-eat-raw-meat

Other Resources:

Holistic Pet Care - Traditional & Holistic Veterinary Services
https://www.holistic-pet-care.com/about-us.html

Natural Herbs That Are Safe For Cats And Dogs
https://homescapepets.com/blogs/articles/natural-herbs-that-are-safe-for-cats-and-dogs

Index

A

Aam (toxins), 43, 113
abscesses, 136
absorption (of nutrients), 123
Abyssinian (cat), 106
acids, 43
adaptogen, 122
adaptogenic, 75
Aghori, 65
Agni (low), 113
alkalized water, 33
allergic reaction, 129
allergies, 111, 122
alligators, 13
Amrutadi *(herbal supplement)*, 62
Amrutas *(herbal supplement)*, 62
Ancient Secrets, vi, x, xv, 4, 14, 26, 77
Ancient Secrets Community, x, xviii
Ancient Secrets Cookbook, Ray, xiii
Ancient Secrets for Kids, Aden, Rogers, xiv
Ancient Secrets Foundation, 64
Ancient Secrets of a Master Healer, Rogers, v, xii, 2, 38, 113
anemia, 121, 149
Angel (dog), 26
Animal Poison Control Center, 131
animal rescue, 42
anti-allergenic, 122
anti-bacterial, 121, 129
antibiotic, 129
anti-depressant, 75
anti-fungal, 121, 129
anti-inflammatory, 121, 132
anti-itching, 122
antioxidants, 132
Anulom *(herbal supplement)*, 62
anxiety, 104, 122
 - separation anxiety, 129
apples, 143
arthritis, 61, 104

Asafetida, 46
Ashtakarma/Panchakarma, 102
Ashwagandha, 75–76
aspartame (unsafe), 152
asthma, 111
Asthtaloc *(herbal supplement)*, 22
Atithi Devo Bhava, 28, 78
Australia, 16
avocados, 143
Ayurcid *(herbal supplement)*, 51
Ayurveda, 103, 104
Ayurvedic herbs, 18
Ayushakti Herbal Supplements, 1, 31, 51
 - Amrutadi, 62
 - Amrutas, 62
 - Anulom, 62
 - Asthtaloc, 22
 - Ayurcid, 51
 - Blis, 62
 - Divyaswas Jivan, 22
 - Gasmukti, 62
 - Granthihar, 51
 - Hartone, 22
 - Immuno, 52
 - Kaishore Guggul, 51, 60
 - Painmukti M.J., 51, 62
 - Painmukti Sandhical, 51, 62
 - Rasnadi Guggul, 51
 - Sandhiyog, 62
 - Sepnil Cream, 60
 - Skin Tonic, 51, 60
 - Skin Tonic Cream, 60
 - Sudarun Lotion, 60
 - Suniram, 60
 - Virechan, 60
 - Virofight, 52
Ayushakti Malad Clinic, Mumbai, 17

B

Baba Ramdas
- *(quote)*, 35, 48, 92
Baby Big Bird (vulture), 82
bacterial infection, 60
Barrett, Mindy, 93
bee, xvii
bee sting, 128
beet juice, 34
belching, 130
belladonna, 72
Benadryl, 129
Bengal (cat), 106
Bengal Tiger, xvii
Bhej (dampness), 18
biotin, 151
birds, vii, xvii, 7, 77, 78
black pepper, 27, 60
black seed oil, 34
Blis *(herbal supplement)*, 62
bloating, 62
blocks, viii
blood clotting, 121, 128
blood pressure, 121, 152
blood sugar, 133
body type, 104
BPCO (similar to COPD), 22
Brincivalli, Dr. Giovanni, xvii, 22, 32, 84
- *(quote)*, 100
broccoli, 34, 143
Broth, 155
Buddha, 4, 26
burdock root, 34
Bureau of Land Management (BLM), 176
burping, 130
butterflies, 4

C

calcium, 62
cannabis, 124
cardiovascular system, 122
carrots, 143
Catahoula, 36
cat food, xvii
cats, vii, xvii, 4, 42
- Abyssinian, 106
- Bengal, 106
- eye infection, 126
- Siamese, 106
Ceylon cinnamon, 127
cheese, 144
cheetahs, 7
chives (unsafe food), 148
chocolate (unsafe food), 148
Chun Chun Baba, 10
circulatory system, 123, 130
coconut oil, 131
cognition, 122
Coleman Taylor, Peggy, 68
conditions
- abscesses, 136
- allergic reaction, 129
- allergies, 111, 122
- anemia, 121
- anxiety, 104, 122, 132
- arthritis, 62, 104
- asthma, 111
- bee sting, 128
- belching, 130
- bloating, 62
- blood clotting, 121, 128
- burping, 130
- circulation issues, 123
- constipation, 62, 126
- dehydration, 131
- diarrhea, 126, 130
- digestive issues, 104, 123
- dry skin, 137
- ear issues, 127
- epilepsy, 131
- eye infection (cat), 126
- fear, 122
- fits, 131
- fleas, 122
- heart issues, 42
- hives, 129

- immune system (low), 122
- insect bites, 128
- joint problems, 122
- kidney issues, 164
- lactose intolerance, 145
- lipomas, 138
- mast cell tumors, 136
- poisoning, 131
- respiratory issues, 123
- sebaceous cyst, 137
- seizures, 131
- separation anxiety, 129
- shakes, 131
- skin allergies, 104
- skin problems, 122
- stiffness, 62
- stress, 132
- ticks, 122
- tumors, 123
- vomiting, 130
- wasp sting, 128
- yeast infection, 127

constipation, 62, 126
contagious healing, x
cooked bones (unsafe food), 150
coordination, 122
Corbin (dog), 43
coriander, 141
cows, 64, 79
crocodiles, 13
crows, 64, 79
cumin, 141
Cushing's Disease, 26

D

Daisy (kitty), 62
Dalkin, Denny, 39
dehydration, 131
dehydrator, 154, 157
Delmenico, Dr. Dipika, 16
depression, 11
detoxification, 113
detox tabs, 43
diarrhea, 126, 130

diet, 6, 102, 113
dietary recommendations, 2, 139
digestion, 109, 123
digestive issues, 104
diuretic, 121
Divine, 21, 40, 64
Divyaswas Jivan *(herbal supplement)*, 22
dog bite, 40
dog food, xvii, **153**
   - cardiovascular, 158
   - heart-healthy, 159
Dog Psalm, 66
dogs, vii, xvii, 4, 42, 64, 79
Dosha
   - excess, 113
Doshas, 75, 104
dry skin, 137

E

eagles, 13, 84, 110
ear issues, 127
elephants, vii, xvii, 4, 179
emergencies, 87
emergency checklist, 96
Engman, Dr. Susan, 169
epilepsy, 131
Equine Therapy, 74
essential oils, 89, 128
evacuating with pets, 93
eye infection (cat), 126

F

fear, 16, 122
First Aid Kit (for pets), 97
fits, 131
flea repellent, 90
fleas, 122, 128
flea treatment, 97
food allergy, 131

G

garlic (unsafe food), 148
gas, 62

Gasmukti *(herbal supplement)*, 62
gastroenteritis, 149
ghee, 18, 27, 40, 60, 130, 144
ginger, 27, 34, 141
ginger root, 130
goats, 45
Golden Paste, 120
Good Deeds-Light Heart Animal Rescue, 154
Granthihar *(herbal supplement)*, 51
grapes (unsafe food), 148
grief, 170
Guggulu, 75

H

Haritaki, 75
Hartone *(herbal supplement)*, 22
hawks, 110
heart issue, 42
herbal formulas, 113
herbal remedies, xvii, 4, 31
herbal supplements, 6, 12, 26, 102
herbs, 2
 - Ayurvedic, 18
hives, 129
Holy Basil, 27
home remedies, 4, 6, 12, 26, 102, 113
Home Remedy for Tumors, 27
honey, 130
honeybees, 4
horses, vii, xvii, 4, 68
Husky, 60

I

ID tag, 97
imbalances, viii
immunity-boosting, 122
Immuno *(herbal supplement)*, 52, 60
infertility, 11
inflammation, 110
insect bites, 128
insecticides, 131
insects, xvii

Integrated Veterinary Care Journal, 105

J

Jivaka, 26
 - see Master Jivaka
Jivanjog *(herbal supplement)*, 31, 84
Jivan Rakshak *(herbal supplement)*, 32
Jnaneddrajii, 10
joey (baby kangaroo), 19, 20

K

Kaishore Guggul *(herbal supplement)*, 51, 60
kangaroos, xvii, 13, 19
Kapha (Dosha), 9, 75, 104
kefir, 144
kibble
 - homemade, 154
kidney failure, 152
kidney issues, 164
Kitchari, 62

L

lactose intolerance, 145
Laksha, 75
laminitis, 72
lavender oil, 129
leeks (unsafe food), 148
leopards, 7
Lieske, Levi, 33
lifestyle, 6, 102
lifestyle changes, 113
lifestyle secrets, 4
lionesses, 7
lions, 4, 7, 110
lipomas, 138
liver problems, 132
Los Angeles, 41
love, 14
Love is the Only Truth, Dalkin, 39
Lowe, Lisa, 40, 153

M

Mamacita (ewe), 45
mantra, 4, 14, 15, 82
maple syrup, 133
Marmaa, 6, 15, 61, 102
Marmaa Shakti, 4, 43, 113
Martino (dog), 32
mast cell tumors, 136
Master Jivaka, 1
- *(quote)*, 86
memory, 122
metabolism, 109
Michael, 26
Mickey (horse), 70
Mike, 65
milk thistle, 132
Milo (dog), vi, 28
- *(photo)*, 30
Miracle Experience Experiment, 64
monkeys, vii, 13
moong beans, 62
moong flour, 156
Mother Teresa *(quote)*, 124
Mumbai, 7
mushrooms, wild (unsafe food), 149
muzzle, 97

N

Naram, Dr. Krushna, xv, xvi, 4
Naram, Dr. Pankaj, vi, xv, xvii, 3, 5, 6, 13, 16, 41, 84, 113
- *(photo)*, 85
- *(quote)*, 24, 40, 114
Naram, Dr. Smita, xv, 5, 6
Naths, 65
natural remedies, 131
neem, 121
Nepal Orphan Kids, 175
nuts (unsafe food), 148

O

Oakley (dog), 49
oat straw, 132
omega 3 oil, 73
Om Namo, Bhagavate, Vasudevaya, 82
Om Sham Namaha, 14
onions (unsafe food), 148
Osi (dog), 36
owls, vii, 13

P

Painmukti M.J. *(herbal supplement)*, 51, 62
Painmukti Sandhical *(herbal supplement)*, 51, 62
panchakarma, 4, 6, 113
panic attacks, 76
panthers, 110
parasites, 60
parsley, 34
Pashupatinath Ashram, 65
Pashupatinath Dogs, 65
peas, 143
pet food, xvii, **142**
phenobarbital, 132
Pitta (Dosha), 9, 36, 75, 104
Pittashamak *(herbal supplement)*, 31
placebo effect, vi
principles, 13
prunes, 126
pulse, 20, 43, 61
pulse reading, 8
pumpkin, 126, 144
pumpkin seeds, 144
python, 4, 13

R

rabbits, xvii, 22
radish, 34
Raktabandha *(herbal supplement)*, 31
Rasnadi Guggul *(herbal supplement)*, 51
rat poison, 131
raw eggs (unsafe food), 150
Ray, Carol K., xvi, xviii, 78
Ray, Elissa, 23

Reiki, 141
Reiki Master, 38
Remedies for Pets, 125
reptiles, xvii
respiratory system, 123, 130
Rogers, Dr. *Clint G.*, **v**, xvii, 1, 28, 38, 65, 79, 113
 - *(Photo)*, 30
Rosco (dog), 33
rose geranium oil, 128

S

safflower oil, 73
Sandhiyog *(herbal supplement)*, 32, 62
Santana (horse), 74
schizophrenia, vii
sebaceous cyst, 137
seeds (unsafe food), 148
seizures, 42, 131
separation anxiety, 129
Sepnil Cream *(Ayushakti)*, 60
sesame seeds, 62
shakes, 131
Shalihotra Samhita, 75
Shankhpushpi *(herbal supplement)*, 76
sheep, 45
Sheru (dog), 61
Siamese, 106
Siddha-Veda, 2, 103
Siddha-Veda lineage, 26
Six Instruments of Siddha-Veda, 102
skin allergies, 104
skin infections, 122
Skin Tonic *(herbal supplement)*, 51, 60
Skin Tonic Cream *(Ayushakti)*, 60
sleep disorders, 76
snakes, vii, 7, 16, 110
 - venomous, 16
Soni, Vinay, 60
spices (dog-safe), 141
 - coriander
 - cumin
 - ginger
 - turmeric
spinach, 34
stamina, 111
stiffness, 62
stomach issues, 130
street dogs, 64
stress, 122, 132
Sudarun Lotion *(Ayushakti)*, 60
sunflower oil, 73
Suniram *(herbal supplement)*, 60
swelling, 129

T

Taylor, Jayna, 49
30-Day Miracle Experiment Game, ix, 29
thrombocytopenia, 31
ticks, 122, 128
tigers, vii, 4, 7, 110
tissues, 113
toxicity, 131
toxins, 43
triphala, 75, 123
triphala powder, 130
Tulsi, 121
tumors, 26, 123
turkey baster, 34
turmeric, 27, 62, 73, 120, 141
turmeric powder, 61

U

ubrication, 111
United States Forest Service (USFS), 176
Unsafe Foods
 - aspartame, 152
 - chives, 148
 - chocolate
 - cooked bones, 150
 - garlic, 148
 - grapes, 148
 - leeks, 148

- mushrooms (wild), 149
- nuts, 148
- onions, 148
- raw egg, 150
- seeds, 148
- xylitol, 152

V

valerian, 132
Vata (Dosha), 9, 20, 63, 75, 104
Veterinary Herbal Medicine, 105
veterinary medicine, 104
Virechan *(herbal supplement)*, 60
Virofight *(herbal supplement)*, 52
vitamins, 143, 151
vomiting, 130
vultures, 78

W

wasp sting, 128
Wechsler, Dr. Stephen, 59
Wildhorse Fire Brigade, 176
Wildlife SOS, 179
Wilkinson, Ann, 70
wolves, 13

X

xylitol (toxic), 127, 131, 152

Y

yeast infection, 127
yogurt, 144

Ancient Secrets Community

For additional information, videos, and to share your animals and pet stories:
https://MyAncientSecrets.com/pets/

Contact us:
For comments, questions, or inquiries:
Team@MyAncientSecrets.com

For Shopping or more:
Products | Ancient Secrets Foundation
https://AncientSecretsFoundation.org/shop/

For additional information:
Discover - Ancient Secrets of a Master Healer
www.MyAncientSecrets.com

192--|-- Ancient Secrets For Pets

Book Cover Design
Courtesy of Maryam Khalifah

Illustrator for children's books, cover art, chapter books, and editorial projects

http://www.maryamartillustration.com

Notes and Health Records

Notes and Health Records

Notes and Health Records

www.ingramcontent.com/pod-product-compliance
Lightning Source LLC
Chambersburg PA
CBHW070137080526
44586CB00015B/1732